DESIGN YOUR LIFE

DESIGN YOUR LIFE

The Pleasures and Perils of Everyday Things

ELLEN AND JULIA LUPTON

ILLUSTRATIONS BY ELLEN LUPTON

ST. MARTIN'S GRIFFIN

NEW YORK

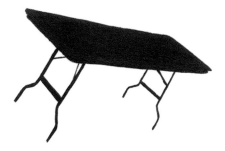

DESIGN YOUR LIFE: THE PLEASURES AND PERILS OF EVERYDAY THINGS

For information, address
St. Martin's Press
175 Fifth Avenue
New York, N.Y. 10010

www.stmartins.com

Library of Congress Cataloging-in-Publication Data
available upon request.

ISBN-13: 978-0-312-53273-4
ISBN-10: 0-312-53273-3

First Edition: May 2009

10 9 8 7 6 5 4 3 2 1

CONTENTS

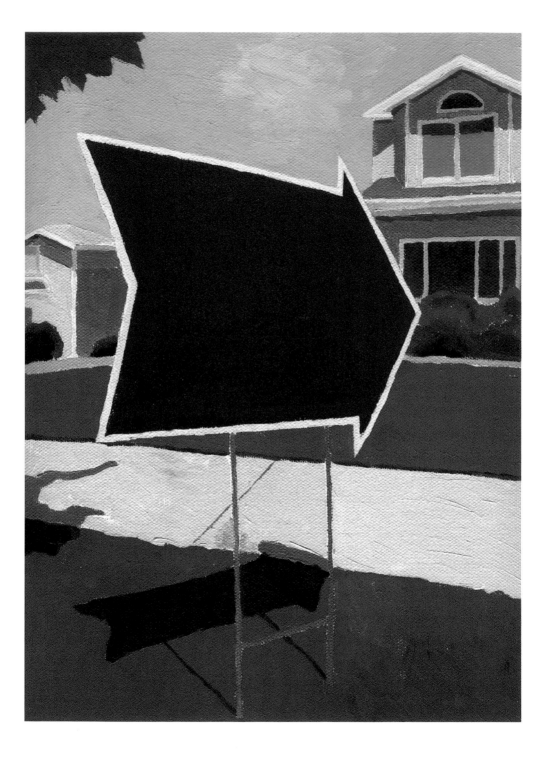

ABOUT THIS BOOK

Find out what's wrong with the bras, pillows, potted plants, festive cookware, and other hopeless stuff you use, buy, clean, water, or put away each day. Discover how to control the actions of those around you by placing objects carefully. Learn why the living room refuses to disappear, and how the arrangement of furniture, hospital rooms, and your own house might be making you miserable. Unlock the power of putting off until tomorrow what you could do today. Find out how one-eyed Siamese bunnies are rebuilding civilization, and how roller bags are threatening to destroy it. Use the tools of self-publishing to take the power of branding into your own hands and communicate with friends, family, and the world.

"Design" is more than the stuff you buy at high-end stores or the modern look that moves products at Target and IKEA. Design is *critical thinking*. It is a way of looking at the world and wondering why things work, and why they don't. Use design to recognize the forms of pleasure and productivity hiding in the messes of daily life, be it a room, a laundry bin, a pile of papers, or a busy schedule. Design is *creative thinking*. Use it to stage memorable parties without burning out, to squeeze meaning and joy out of commercial holidays, and to enact your own vision of what's hip, cool, beautiful, or just.

Design Your Life is about objects and how we interact with them. Illustrated throughout with paintings of things both ordinary and odd, this book casts a sharp eye on parenthood, housekeeping, entertaining, time management, crafting, and more. We take an irreverent and realistic look at everything from the objects on our counters and the rooms we live in to the attitudes that promise us happiness in an increasingly fragile world. Speaking to readers who are both design-conscious and consumer-wary, *Design Your Life* taps into the popular interest in design as well as people's desire to make their own way through a mass-produced world.

Ellen and Julia Lupton

HERE AND THERE

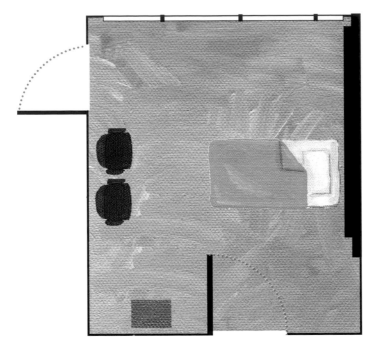

BEFORE

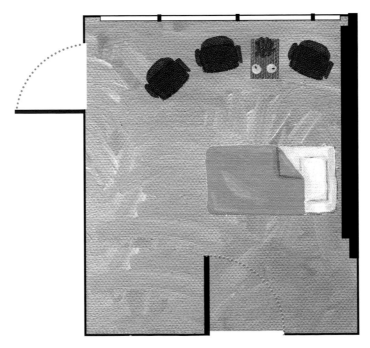

AFTER

MOVING THE FURNITURE

I found myself in a narrow room. Two vinyl-covered armchairs faced the foot of my bed; a small steel table on wheels was stationed in a far corner. Was it a minimum security prison for inside traders? No, it was the hospital room where I was sent to rest after delivering my second baby. Holding my newborn daughter against my chest and grateful for the basic comforts of this ordinary room, I didn't give a second thought to how it was designed.

My husband Abbott, however, paced around the room, seeing flaws in its arrangement and seeking ways to improve it. He brings this creative and critical eye everywhere he goes. At his sister's house one holiday, he reshuffled the light bulbs in the living room, changing the wattage in each lamp to make the setting more sociable—brighter here, dimmer there. Invited to lecture at a university, he realigned a rigid battalion of chairs into relaxed, staggered waves.

Here in this hospital room, our son would meet his baby sister for the first time, and my parents would hold their newest granddaughter. The poorly sited armchairs would have placed our guests at the end of my weary body, so Abbott moved them near the window and alongside the bed. He commandeered an extra chair from the hallway and added it to this newly assembled seating area. The steel table migrated there as well, providing a resting spot for cups of coffee and cans of Coke as well as a vase of flowers.

As I cradled our sleeping daughter in my arms, I watched an indifferently planned space become a room that welcomed visitors and encouraged lingering and conversation.

Ten years later, the kids and I have learned a lot from Abbott's penchant for moving furniture. Although we are sometimes mystified by his constant attention to how things are arranged, in the end, he nearly always succeeds in making the spaces we live in brighter, or more comfortable, or simply refreshed and renewed. Change, in itself, keeps our rooms alive.

"Daddy is a poltergeist," I say to our kids, explaining how massive pieces of furniture have managed to move from room to room while we were out playing at the park.

"Daddy has a furniture problem," I declare, as Abbott enters the house one Sunday heaving along two vintage Florence Knoll end tables and a George Nelson desk purchased from a local antique dealer.

"They had just arrived in the store when I got there," he exclaims, glowing with exertion and delight.

"How much?"

"Not cheap."

"Where will they go?"

"I'll find a place."

A clunky ballet ensues as tables, chairs, and sofas seek alternate lodging throughout the house, where they enjoy new lives in new locations. Many people avoid moving furniture, putting in place their couch, chairs, coffee table, and lamps, and leaving them there for years, even a lifetime. The furniture melts into the floor and becomes invisible. My maternal grandmother lived in several different homes when I was growing up, and she managed to arrange the furniture the same way wherever she went. It was as if she hadn't moved at all.

In the Middle Ages and Renaissance, domestic spaces were reconfigured daily, with one large room accommodating work, meals, and sleep. The French word for "furniture" is *meubles,* meaning "moveable"; Spanish is *muebles,* Italian is *mobili,* and Portuguese is *mobiliário.* Chairs are the ultimate moveable furnishings, easily reconfigured to create circles of conversation or rows of attention. Portable folding chairs date from antiquity.

In our era of more frozen floor plans, rezoning often occurs as families expand and contract—adding new members, adapting to changing abilities and disabilities, expelling grown children and absorbing aging parents. But furniture needn't wait for major life changes in order to be moved. When we recently shifted a marble coffee table from one sitting area to another, we discovered that the piece reflects more light in its new setting, subtly changing the entire room.

People who never move their furniture stop seeing their environment. They get used to banging into an awkwardly placed bureau, bruising their shins on it over and over without deciding to shift its position. They avoid sitting in an uncomfortable chair, but don't replace it, and they stop using a drawer that sticks, but don't fix it. A vase or curio waits unnoticed in its cabinet, and works of art fade away into the paint and plaster.

A few years ago, our Baltimore town house became a location for a Hollywood film. Over the course of a week, we saw our rooms transformed not just once but several times. The set decorator, a big bossy blonde from Los Angeles, borrowed chairs, tables, sofas, and beds from furniture stores around the city; most pieces were sent back in failure as she searched for just the right look. As the rooms continued to convulse with furniture, a pattern emerged: although the pieces kept changing, their position stayed more or less the same. A bigger couch superseded a smaller one. A puffy chair with stubby legs supplanted a square one dressed in a box-pleated skirt. What's more, the arrangement of these new pieces duplicated that of our own furnishings. A new dining area appeared exactly where ours had been, with artfully mismatched antiques replacing our modern table and chairs.

The team from Hollywood hadn't *redesigned* our house; they had merely switched out the objects and finishes. The sight lines, traffic patterns, and basic functions had stayed the same. Changing a slipcover to match the drapes isn't design in the most active sense.

Design is *thinking*, materialized in objects and environments, inscribed in patterns of use, and addressed by analysis and planning. A work of design—be it a room, a jacket, or a page—results from deliberate thought. What is it for? What will it cost? How will it be used? Well-designed environments make sense, their beauty often resting in the transparency and accessibility of their functions. Design sometimes means exposing an environment's hidden agenda and making the most of it. If your dining room has become a place where books and papers are stacked, perhaps it's time to turn it into a library. If everyone in the house gravitates to the most comfortable chair, you may want to find other chairs like it. When people allow the functions of a room to ossify, they ignore the power of design.

Do you control your environment, or does your environment control you? Moving the furniture is part of the philosophy of this book. The people in your world can become furniture, too, used but not noticed, made invisible through habit. Your calendar of routines and obligations is a floor plan for the day; make sure that each "room" is serving your needs and pleasures as best it can. At our house, moving the furniture has become a way of pulling happiness and sociability—in place of frustration and boredom—out of ordinary situations, simply by shaking them up a bit. **EL**

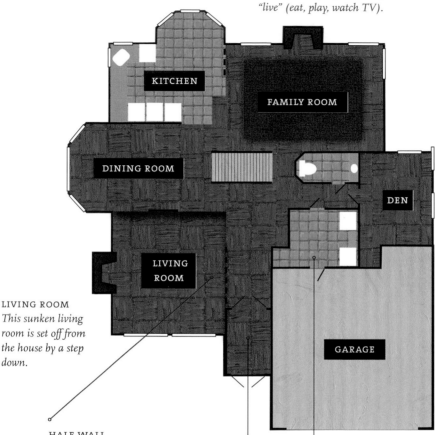

FAMILY ROOM
This is where people actually "live" (eat, play, watch TV).

KITCHEN

FAMILY ROOM

DINING ROOM

DEN

LIVING
ROOM

GARAGE

LIVING ROOM
This sunken living room is set off from the house by a step down.

HALF WALL
A low wall puts room on display while discouraging actual foot traffic. Whereas the Victorian parlor was sealed off with doors, the modern living room has more symbolic borders.

FRONT DOOR
Entrance hall is an atrophied descendent of the medieval great hall, a vast room used for eating, sleeping, and fighting.

GARAGE ENTRANCE
The functional (rather than symbolic) front door is through the garage and laundry room. In this typical floor plan, the garage is by far the home's largest room.

PERSISTENCE OF THE LIVING ROOM *Typical suburban floor plan*

THE DEATH AND LIFE OF THE LIVING ROOM

The living room has been pronounced dead—again. Cause of death: asphyxiation by fabric, furniture, and disuse. Born around 1910 from a venerable line of drawing rooms and parlors, the living room has been survived by the family room, great room, retreat, patio, and SUV. In lieu of flowers, the house asks that you observe a moment of silence on a sofa at your nearest Starbucks.

Every generation proclaims the death of the living room, yet it keeps coming back. We seem to need its empty formality, choosing to preserve a bit of protected, cultivated parkland in the urban centers of our busy houses. The living room is an elephant in the modern dwelling—a large room, often the first one you see, flaunting the home's most cherished furnishings, yet largely ignored in daily life. In order to protect the living room from the slow, terrible death caused by toy infestation and piles of junk mail, home owners and developers have quarantined it with garage room entryways, family room duplications, and sunken designs that isolate it from regular traffic. Periodically, domestic writers (joined by the occasional husband) pronounce the demise of the living room, decrying it as wasted space and conspicuous consumption. Yet these elephants keep butting back into our floor plans. The living room expresses people's desire to mark off a space that is casual enough to afford comfort, formal enough to invite self-expression, and austere enough to resist unwanted clutter.

The mother of the living room is the parlor, which enjoyed its heyday in the Victorian era. The nineteenth-century parlor sat at the front of the house, but in its own cage, safely hidden behind a door just off the entrance hall. Wrapped in factory fabrics and stuffed with collectibles, the parlor was a museum of memories. The parlor concept quickly spread to the apartments, balconies, and even tents of working people, thanks to the furniture ensemble known as the parlor suite, a sitting area grouped around a small table. The sofa still performs this parlorizing function today, popping up in waiting rooms, cafés, and offices as a symbol of domestic comfort and hospitality.

Between 1900 and 1930, the word "living room" replaced "parlor." Along with the new name came a more open floor plan inspired by the modernism of the Arts and Crafts movement. Yet formality crept back in, and the living room soon froze once more into a precious precinct of order. Beginning in the 1950s, the family room and the great room emerged as warmer alternatives, and for a while, the living room seemed to be going extinct, forced out of the domestic ecosystem by these more relaxed and resilient spaces.

But the open plan of the family room or great hall breeds its own dangers. With everything from cooking and eating to homework and home offices happening in one sprawling area, heaps of paper and baskets of toys build up quickly. The messiness of the open plan in turn elicits the home dweller's desire to restore a pocket of order.

And so the living room keeps returning. My own living room, which vaunts a cathedral ceiling and a bank of double-height windows, is the only architectural gesture in our southern California tract house. We've reduced the furniture to two modern benches, a side board, and a bank of CDs. It functions more as a foyer than a sitting room, but we enter its well-lit space every day, through the front door. Its austerity may discourage immediate use, but the very emptiness of the room performs a mental function for the whole house. It is a physical embodiment of repose amidst the whirl of daily activity. Our living room, I've decided, is like a sleeping cat, whose idle purring inserts a quiet rhythm into the busy biology of the household. Like our cats, our living room sustains us simply by doing nothing at all. **JL**

LIVING ROOM *Elephant in the house*

Talking Points

The living room is a public space, not a private one. It's an area where people gather, perhaps every day on an informal basis, or—in more rigid and spacious houses—only on holidays, funerals, and in-law visitations. Many things go on in modern living rooms, including reading, snacking, watching television, listening to music, and drinking large or small quantities of alcohol.

The activity that has traditionally defined the living room is conversation. The choice and placement of furniture, the character of the lighting, and the overall sound, color, and ambience are all designed to get people talking. Sofas and chairs are angled and spaced to keep bodies close, but not uncomfortably so. Flat surfaces permit the display of objects as well as the serving of snacks. Shelves of books absorb sound (so that you can hear the person next to you); they also offer a ready reserve of conversation topics. Fireplaces provide a visual focal point as well as an expression of warmth (even if the real heat is coming from a radiator or from thy neighbor's thigh). Today, many households are apt to replace their fireplace with a large-scale TV set, while orienting their furniture more for viewing than for talking—but even television is more fun when watched with other people.

Interior designers advocate three kinds of lighting for most rooms: general illumination, typically reflected off the walls or ceiling; task lighting for reading, knitting, or making paperclip chains; and accent lighting for showing off works of art. A room equipped only with general illumination will feel dull and flat, whereas a room lit only with lamps will be dark overall, punctuated by stingy dabs of brightness. Local lighting provides sparkle and contrast within a generally lit room. **EL**

FUNCTIONAL FURNITURE GROUPING

Dysfunctional Furniture Groupings

Interior designers and feng shui enthusiasts have generated a wealth of guidance about how to arrange furniture to achieve social harmony and inner peace. But what about households who would rather be miserable—or who gather together only under threat of punishment?

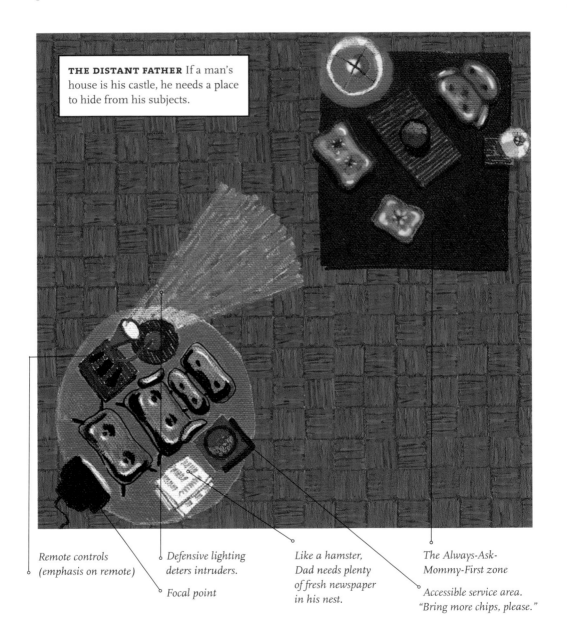

THE DISTANT FATHER If a man's house is his castle, he needs a place to hide from his subjects.

Remote controls (emphasis on remote)

Defensive lighting deters intruders.

Focal point

Like a hamster, Dad needs plenty of fresh newspaper in his nest.

The Always-Ask-Mommy-First zone

Accessible service area. "Bring more chips, please."

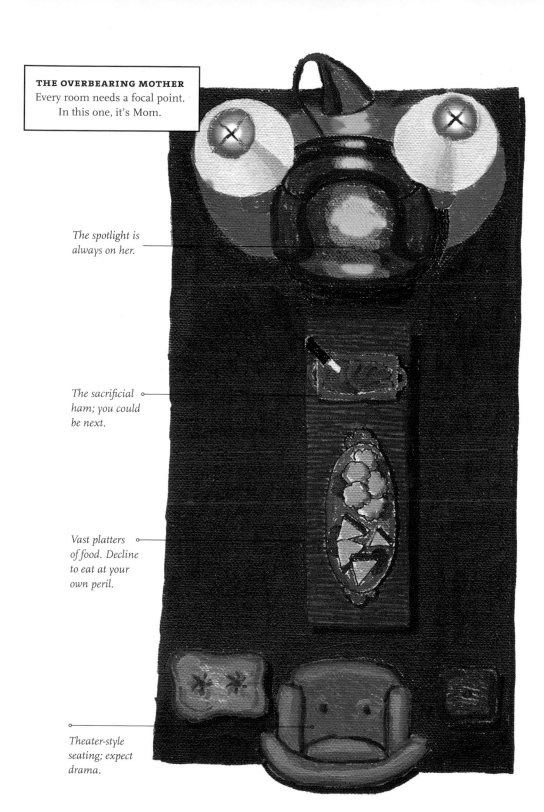

THE OVERBEARING MOTHER
Every room needs a focal point.
In this one, it's Mom.

The spotlight is
always on her.

The sacrificial
ham; you could
be next.

Vast platters
of food. Decline
to eat at your
own peril.

Theater-style
seating; expect
drama.

INSIDE OR OUTSIDE? *The Dutch designer Petra Blaisse created this yellow silk curtain to hang inside an exhibition (designed by Rem Koolhaas/OMA at the Museum Boijmans Van Beuningen, 1989). The curtain is blown by artificial wind, producing an exquisite illusion of contact with the outside world.*

VIEW FINDINGS

Hard-core minimalists abhor curtains, preferring to keep their windows bare under nearly any circumstance. (When absolutely necessary, install blinds.) Yet curtains are functional as well as decorative, regulating light, privacy, climate, and sound, as well as defining physical space in a flexible way. Curtains are also, of course, decorative, bringing color, texture, and pattern. Buildings are fixed, but curtains move. They pull open and shut, they billow in the breeze, and they change transparency as the sun shifts. These soft complements to hard architecture are sensual in every sense of the word—they shape our lived, bodily experience of a space, not just visually, but through touch, sound, and temperature. Curtains can represent a substantial outlay of time and money, and yet they are by nature temporary, destined to dissolve, eventually, under the rays of the sun. (Meanwhile, they can guard your furniture against similar decline.)

Choosing draperies or sewing them at home is an area where women have customarily held sway, along with other soft-goods decisions like pillows and bed linens. Women have been the artists and inventors of the modern curtain, turning this humble medium into an experimental form, as seen in countless home decorating guides as well as in high-end installations by curtain innovators such as Lilly Reich, Mary Bright, and Petra Blaisse, who have constructed curtains using unusual materials and techniques. Blaisse, who designs gardens as well as curtains, sees the trees and grasses outdoors as elements of window treatment, since they affect light, shade, and view inside the building.

A window is a frame, and a curtain is a frame around a frame. What do frames do, and why do we need them? Frames separate works of art from the ordinary world. A frame can be thick or thin, light or dark. It can meld with the environment or blend with the image it supports. Contemporary art galleries often dispense with pedestals and picture moldings, and yet the white, open space of the gallery is itself a frame that announces art's special status. A well-designed curtain doesn't hide the window, but rather dramatizes it, calling attention to the presence of the outside world. Sometimes, it creates the illusion of a window when none is there. **EL**

THE MODERN CURTAIN, 1927

Lilly Reich designed this interior for a model apartment building in Germany. (The building was designed by Ludwig Mies van der Rohe, with whom she was a frequent collaborator.) Here, a floor-to-ceiling drapery serves as a flexible room divider, while translucent panels diffuse light from the outside. Reich designed the curtains as well as the tubular steel furniture pieces.

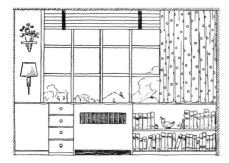

THE MODERN CURTAIN, 1946

Many inspiring decorating books were published in the mid-twentieth century. These books delivered modernist design ideas to homemakers and college girls. One of our favorites is *Popular Home Decoration*, by Mary Davis Gillies. The designs shown here use curtains with extra length and width to enhance the apparent size of the windows. Similar techniques are employed in many contemporary hotel rooms, where a wall of drapes helps make a small window with an ugly view of the parking lot look sweeping and dramatic.

THE MODERN CURTAIN, 2000

Curtains don't have to be all the same length. Designer Mary Bright worked with numerous architects and interior designers at the turn of the twenty-first century to create stunning window treatments like this one for a New York City restaurant. Overlapping panels of sheer fabric hang from thin chains. She often used unorthodox materials such as paper, rubber, leather, metal mesh, and teflon-coated nylon. Bright, who began her career as a milliner, was an expert seamstress as well as designer. She died of cancer in 2002 at age 48.

Curtain Calls

Just like people, not all windows look better naked. The length and width of a curtain, like the cut of a jacket or a dress, changes the way a window is perceived. Different styles can make a plain-Jane window look amorous, glamorous, extravagant—or downright dowdy. Modern curtains tend to hang long and straight. They are translucent rather than opaque, serving to diffuse light rather than to block it.

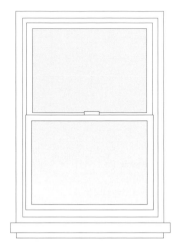

NUDE

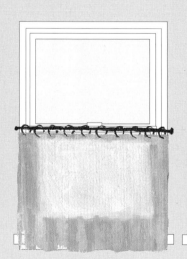

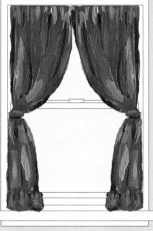

TOPLESS *Functional, not frilly, the café curtain is an easy start for those who are drapery-adverse. Covering just half your window provides privacy while letting in lots of light.*

HAUS FRAU *This old-fashioned look is coming back (along with fluffy skirts, flirty aprons, and frosted cupcakes). Falling just above the sill, the short, perky cut of this curtain emphasizes the window's inherent body shape.*

LIKE A VIRGIN *Sheer fabric panels diffuse light and eliminate glare, creating a luminous field in place of a harsh, bright hole in the wall. Sheer panels that hang a little wider and longer than the frame will enhance the apparent size of the window opening. A white-on-white pattern adds interest without changing the color of the room.*

CLASSIC CENTER PART

COMB-OVER

ELVIS

A draped valance or a tailored cornice serves to create an illusion of height or obscures hardware. Like a hair extension or a comb-over, a valance is primarily about illusion.

BRIDE OF FRANKENSTEIN

FARRAH FAWCETT

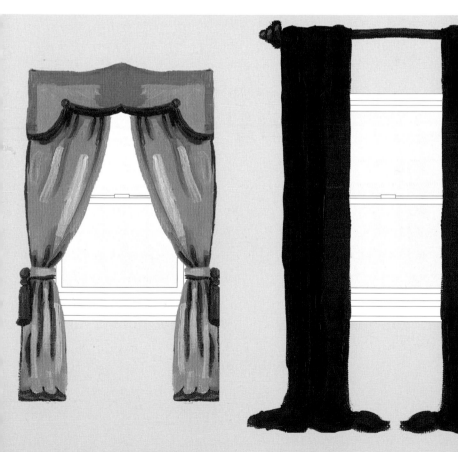

PRINCESS *It's draperies like these that give curtains a bad name.*

DIVA *Tall panels of fabric fall into puddles on the ground, projecting an aura of glamour and an illusion of height.*

Why Is the Clown Sad?

Works of art are deeply personal elements of the domestic interior. A well chosen and well cared for artwork could be part of your family legacy for generations. Yet any painting or photograph will suffer if it is poorly installed. Shown here are some common mistakes that are easily avoided with attention to basic design principles: scale, balance, simplicity, and hierarchy.

Avoid overpowering a delicate work of art with a heavy, ornate frame.

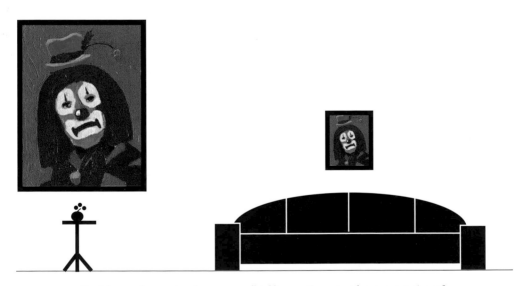

Don't hang a large artwork over a small table, or a tiny artwork over a massive sofa.

*Never arrange art in a stair step pattern
except over stairs.*

*Don't make works of art compete
with a carnival of curios.*

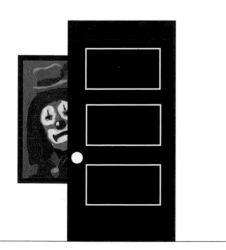

*Don't obscure art behind a door
that is usually left open.*

*Never hang objects over a child's bed,
especially not a large, depressing object.*

THE NEO PORCH *Nicer than a garage facade, but can it really deliver the neighborliness it promises?*

PORCH ENVY

I live on a cul-de-sac in Southern California. Built in 1989, the facades on our street are swallowed up by the great beige blankness of garage doors. When my children were very young, the neighbors and I would sit at the shadeless edges of our driveways wearily watching our toddlers play in the asphalt circle. A porch retreat would have been welcome (a baby sitter even more so).

On an adjacent street, built just a few years later, the porch is back, part of the New Urbanism, a movement to create denser, more social suburban neighborhoods. Garages have scooted discreetly to the sides of the houses, and modest verandas frame the front doors. Yet some of these porches are so small they are really just covered entry ways. Some have been left completely unfurnished, not even pretending to fulfill a greater social function. Others had dreamed once of becoming container gardens, but have degraded instead into gardening sheds, complete with fertilizer bags, muddy trowels, and tangled hoses. Many porches serve as storage units for bikes, strollers, and scooters—second garages for secondary vehicles. The most successful porches are those that form an L. The side piece, served by an additional doorway and set back from the street, is more likely to shelter a cluster of furniture (although I have seen no one sitting there).

Unlike the voluptuous verandas of older houses, new porches are often too skinny to seat a real gathering, let alone a broken washing machine. As for leisure, people may mingle more freely at the local café or in common areas like the park or the pool than in front of their houses. And if television first drew people off the veranda and into the living room, the Internet has social charms that no sidewalk can provide. Facebook is the new front porch.

Along with balconies the size of window boxes and driveways paved like patios, these narrow newcomers may prove to be more a symptom of gas-and-electric life than a solution to it. Still, some people actually do use their porches. One Santa Monica friend reports using her porch as a smoking gallery and overflow space during parties. Another friend, who lives in a New Urban development outside Indianapolis, is never bored on her porch; she brings her wireless laptop outside with her.

Landscape architect Andrew Jackson Downing taught Americans how to grow porches around their houses like vines.

Andrew Jackson Downing (1815–1852) popularized the rural cottage, and with it the porch, as the signature of American vernacular housing. According to Downing, the porch invites, prepares, and shelters the visitor. A country house without a porch, he declared, is like a "book without a title page, leaving the stranger to plunge *in medias res*, without the friendly preparation of a single word of introduction." Trained as a landscape gardener in the picturesque style, Downing treated the porch as an ornamental, organic form that could wind around and knit together the straight angles of the building, while also opening the inside to the outside, the cottage to its garden.

Downing promoted the rural cottage for middle-class home owners through his widely distributed pattern books. Architect and urban planner Christopher Alexander reinvented the pattern idea in his 1977 text, *A Pattern Language: Towns, Buildings, Construction*. This thick little volume recalls the pattern books of yore; designed to travel easily between classrooms and construction sites, Alexander's book features dense pages of old-fashioned typography peppered with tiny black and white drawings.

For Alexander, a pattern is not a floor plan, but rather a connecting principle that links up places and populations via physical behaviors and activities. Patterns such as "old people everywhere," "accessible green," and "local sports" profess the value of mixed use, diverse populations, and neighborhood networks. While building a house means considering the surrounding locale, creating a kitchen mobilizes such patterns as "eating atmosphere," "pool of light," and "child caves." The house is a node, not a thing, a moment in a flow of people, goods, and actions that ultimately connects us all.

"People are different sizes; they sit in different ways. . . .
Never furnish any place with chairs that are identically
the same." —Christopher Alexander, 1977
Drawing by Jennifer Tobias

So, too, for Alexander a porch is not a thing added to a house as a pocket or collar might be attached to a dress. Instead, a successful porch brings together a cluster of social uses and habits. The porch is composed of such patterns as "private terrace on the street," "sunny place," "outdoor room," "raised flowers," and "different chairs." Out of these patterns, something we might call "porchness" takes shape, involving elements of openness, enclosure, shade, a relationship to the road, and some places to sit.

A few deeply practical tips come out of Alexander's analysis, such as the dictum that if a porch is really an outdoor room, it should be at least six feet deep, to accommodate a small table and chairs. (Neo-porches, on the other hand, are often skinny appendages or inflated facades that barely afford a bench.) The porch is also a conversation with the neighborhood—it's not strictly private, but communicates with passersby. There is an economy to Alexander's pattern poetry: if you put pots of flowers on your porch, you might not need them elsewhere. And if the front porch functions as a terrace on the street, you may not yearn for a patio out back.

I asked a friend from the next block, a sexy scientist from Argentina, how she uses her new porch. "I don't actually sit out there," she said, "but it's great for package delivery. You know"—her voice dropped into a confidential quiver—"from Victoria's Secret and Frederick's of Hollywood." I am glad that the neo-porch is enhancing the sex lives of working mothers, but it hasn't yet revived the social world framed by its historic ancestors. Maybe I shouldn't feel so bad about not having a porch. Perhaps all I need is a new blog, a raspberry frappuccino, or a Really Special Delivery. **JL**

Porch History

The porticos of antiquity fronted public buildings. In Africa, porch-like structures provided shelter from sun and insects, while opening onto a shared common area. The American house porch is an amalgam of European, African, and Indian imports. Killed by television, air-conditioning, and the garage, the porch has been revived by New Urbanism. Garages have shifted to the sides of the houses, and modest verandas now frame the front doors of many new homes. Yet these under-used add-ons may be more symbolic of social activity than truly a habitat for it.

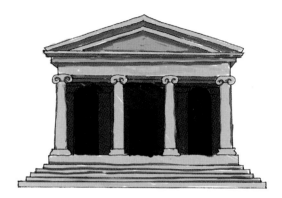

500 BC GREEK STOA *The Greek stoa was a colonnade around a temple. Later, colonnades were used in front of civic buildings, for conducting business in public. The columns offered transparency before the witnessing citizens. The Roman portico served a similar function.*

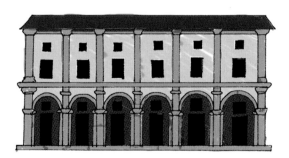

1433 FLORENTINE PALAZZO *The loggia, following the Greek stoa and Roman portico, was initially associated in the Renaissance with public buildings. On commercial streets, loggia protected and unified the sidewalk in front of ground floor storefronts, creating the first pedestrian malls.*

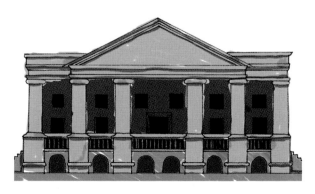

1570 PALLADIO'S LOGGIA *Palladio adopted the loggia for the villas of aristocrats, its first major domestic use—but by no means a vernacular one (unlike the American porch).*

1500 EUROPE-INDIA CONTACT *In India, the veranda is designed to cool the air and provide extra living space. British colonials quickly adopted the idea, creating their own mega-bungalows with verandas.*

1650 SLAVE DWELLINGS IN BRAZIL *When slaves got off the boat in Brazil, their first job was to erect their own housing. Note the thatched overhang that extends living space into a shared public area.*

1880 VICTORIAN FRONT PORCH *Steps create distance between the house and sidewalk and elevate the seated homeowner, nurturing a feeling of security.*

1985 FRONT PORCH; FRONT GARAGE *Porches poured from concrete and hugging the ground are essentially patios with banisters, making easy transitions for strollers, wheelchairs, and drunken guests.*

2008 FRONT PORCH; SIDE GARAGE *The classic American porch extends most of the length of the facade. Suburban houses in the 1970s and 80s made the garage the most prominent feature of the house. Today, porches are coming back. But what are they really used for?*

CRAVING THE BUZZ *It's not just the coffee that's addictive; it's the comfort of strangers.*

GETTING OUT OF THE HOUSE

In his book *The Great Good Place*, sociologist Ray Oldenburg mounted a best-selling defense of what he called the Third Place, "public places that host the regular, voluntary, informal, and happily anticipated gathering of individuals beyond the realm of home and work." His favorite haunts were the French café and the English pub; he decried the exclusion of such spaces from the gated cul-de-sacs and vast residential prairies of American culture.

Since Oldenburg's beer-and-coffee jeremiad first appeared in 1989, mainstream marketing has embraced the Third Place idea with a couch-in-every-corner vengeance. The New Urbanism has scripted various gathering places into its vision for suburban renewal. (Shopping is big. So are health clubs. People go to the gym not just for the equipment, but to enjoy the sweat and struggle of other people.) Meanwhile, in contemporary brandscaping, hip retail outlets masquerade as museums, upscale supermarkets have morphed from obligatory stopping points into festive destinations, and the very smell of coffee has come to signify upscale unwinding.

Most French bistros, writes Oldenburg, have no signage, for the simple reason that they have no names. Starbucks has gone so far in the opposite direction that its ubiquity has finally rendered it generic. Starbucks is not a Third Place. It is a Google Place—a phenomenon that is many zero's greater than the sum of its stores, since it has come to name not only a place and a product, but a global business model (as in "Starbucksification."). Like Jell-O and Kleenex, but with far greater spatial repercussions, Starbucks has reached the ultimate brand destination. The species has renamed the genus.

Another sociologist, R. K. Merton, distinguished between the "manifest function" of social practices (say, drinking coffee) and its "latent function" (call it hanging out). Market researchers aim to disclose the hidden needs fulfilled by existing products in order to deliver a made-to-order service that will target those needs directly. *Voilà*: the latent becomes manifest, and everyone's happy. When an underground phenomenon goes commercial, however, will it still perform its salutary social work with the same spontaneous energy? The long lines for carry-out at my local Starbucks indicate that most of my neighbors are drinking Joe in their cars, not reading Jacques on the banquette.

The process of "going to work" is changing for many people, as more businesses and individuals discover the value of home offices—in 2007, IBM reported that 30 percent of its employees were "mobile." Consultants and freelancers have long worked from home, where routine challenges include fridge avoidance, spousal distraction, and a creeping sense of isolation. Much as home workers value their freedom from water-cooler tyranny, they sometimes crave the buzz of public places. Numerous businesses have sprung up to provide temporary office space to mobile workers, offering them with a place to work, rest, go online, and be in the company of others. A service called "Paragraph" is geared to writers in New York City. The facility combines privacy (each writer gets a cubicle) with a sense of community (the other cubicles contain people pursuing a shared art). Common kitchen and "living" spaces are public areas rimmed by sheltered moments for inward contemplation. Libraries do the same thing for free, and they remain an important gathering place for people of all ages and abilities. (Today, some libraries even let you drink coffee.)

The novelist and essayist Louis Auchincloss has produced an astonishing body of work over the course of his six-decade career. During much of that time, he was employed as an attorney. Yearning to focus on his writing, Auchincloss left his firm for a brief period but found that even with more time and fewer distractions, he wasn't more productive than he had been when formally employed. In fact, he missed the experience of writing quickly during the short gaps between meetings and court appointments. So he returned to his Wall Street lawyer's job—and he kept writing, producing such legendary accounts of New York life and scandal as *The Embezzler* (1966).

I spent my childhood at the local public library and then graduated to the university version. For two decades, I preferred to read and write outside of the house. Now, I abjure public spaces in favor of my kitchen, which is public enough in a house full of kids. I get my best reading done on airplanes, though, where the engine buzz and the fat guy next to me conspire to weave that strange cocoon—that precious knitting of a private space within a public one—that only Third Places supply. Meanwhile, airport bookstores seem to be thriving, their wares providing a portable wall of words for travelers to hide behind. **JL**

SWEAT SHOP *Working out in the company of others.*

OBJECTILE
DYSFUNCTION

BORN AGAIN *Each day, the humble toaster brings the miracle of life to stale bread.*

ARE TOASTERS NECESSARY?

My household once acquired a very beautiful toaster. Ordered from a prominent mail-order purveyor of modern design objects, it was a sleek, elegant monolith manufactured by Rowenta and designed by the brilliant British product designer Jasper Morrison. When the Rowenta Model TL90 arrived on our doorstep, however, total satisfaction did not arrive with it. After liberating it from its packaging and plugging its vinyl-covered tail into our patiently waiting electrical outlet, I tried to make toast. Nothing. No satisfying click of the internal mechanism as I pressed the "touch-sensitive" power button. No warm glow emanating from the wires enclosed inside this graceful obelisk of plastic and chrome. No reassuring smell of burning carbohydrates.

I confess to never having read a toaster manual before, but the TL90 seemed to need one (forty-four pages in seven languages). I soon learned that my toaster had failed to "initialize" (i.e., turn on when plugged in), and it would need to be replaced. So back in the box and off to the customer care clinic it went, giving me two weeks to ponder a burning question: Are toasters necessary? Is civilized life possible without this fundamental kitchen gadget? Could a twenty-first-century family get by with no toaster at all?

Toasted bread is a key component of the Western diet, and for good reason. The toasting process makes old bread better than new, transforming its very molecular structure. As bread goes stale—a process that begins the moment the loaf exits the maternal oven—the water molecules inside the bread begin migrating to the crust, making the outer layer tough and gummy while the interior goes dry. Exposing the bread to high heat disrupts the bonding of the water molecules, restoring the tender, toothsome texture of the outer layer. As the bread burns, the sugars and starches begin to carmelize, becoming sweet, dark, and flavorful.

It turns out that there are numerous ways to make toast, and I tried many of them while awaiting the return of the TL90. An oven broiler works well if you are mindful of burning and you flip the bread to achieve toasting on both sides. A stove-top frying pan allows for easier surveillance and possibly less heat waste than the oven broiler. Indeed, I often "fry" a bagel or sliced baguette after employing the pan for something else, giving the heat and oil already stored there a second tour of duty. The cook who loves danger can toast bread slices directly in the stove's gas flame, while the more cautious pyromaniac will enjoy charring thick slices of bread on an outdoor grill, placing them on a low flame for a few minutes just as the grilled meats are nearing completion. Microwaving bread is, of course, a disaster, as the process agitates the gluten and turns the whole thing into a rubbery wad of over-excited particles.

In contrast with these alternative procedures, an ordinary toaster provides a quick, automated, and predictable means for making toast. Yet even operating a basic toaster requires some measure of skill—hence the prevalence of that burnt bread smell in mornings across America. Why is it so hard to make toast? First, when you activate your toaster, no matter what model, the wires need time to heat up. Impatient cooks ignore this fact, turning the dial up high for the first batch of toast and thus needlessly incinerating the second round. Furthermore, drier slices requires less heat than fresher ones, and any loaf containing sugar, such as raisin bread, burns more rapidly.

Whatever the method, the toasting process is a tiny miracle that has the power, Phoenix-like, to revive our daily bread with its healing fire. As for Jasper Morrison's TL90, we used it for a while before putting it up for adoption. It is wonderful to look at, but despite being as wide as a four-slice toaster, its elegant body has room for only two slices of bread, making it a great gadget for a chic bachelor pad but a poor choice for a family of four. **EL**

THE IPOD OF TOASTERS The sleek Rowenta TL90 was designed by Jasper Morrison. Some users will feel constrained by its two-slice playlist. Morrison's own website posts a warning about consumer reports of malfunctioning. The problems could stem from manufacture rather than design.

MERRY-GO-ROUND Ingenious devices for toasting bread include this rack made around 1800, for use in open fireplaces. After placing a slice of bread between each of the wire arches, the cook pushes the device close to the fire. Halfway through, she pivots the rack to toast the other side of the bread.

DISPLAY MODEL Early electric toasters exposed the wires—and the toasting bread—to view. It later became fashionable to enclose the mechanism inside a streamlined body, which made toasters safer to use if more mysterious and more difficult to clean. This design, c. 1909, includes a rack on top for keeping the finished toast warm. Electric toasters quickly became a standard feature in the modern kitchen.

MRS. JAMES BOND The ordinary countertop toaster is appealing because it does one thing well—making toast. The Back to Basics TEM500 Egg-and-Muffin Two-Slice Toaster and Egg Poacher (or the Hot Diggety Dogger electric hot dog cooker) may go too far in the direction of product specialization, adding a function whose singularity borders on the absurd.

THE MINIVAN OF TOASTERS It's not pretty, but it gets you there. The toaster oven has a big footprint but it performs many functions. Use it for reviving stale baguettes, obsolete pizza, and various strips, sticks, and nuggets of frozen food. Some users find the dual toast/bake controls confusing, but if you can learn to drive a Dodge Caravan, you can certainly master a toaster oven.

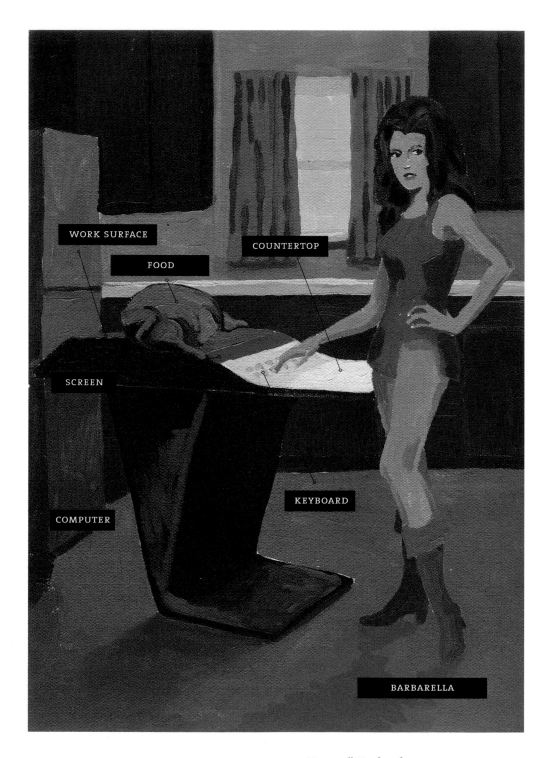

WORK SURFACE

FOOD

COUNTERTOP

SCREEN

COMPUTER

KEYBOARD

BARBARELLA

THE FIRST KITCHEN COMPUTER *Honeywell H316, 1969*

COMPUTER IN THE KITCHEN

The first computer designed for the kitchen was manufactured by Honeywell in 1969. A swooping console equipped with a countertop, keypad, and a tiny, narrow screen, the H316 was as big as a washing machine and did little more than archive recipes. At $10,000, it retailed for roughly the same price as a tract house. This spectacle of space-age modernity failed, not surprisingly, to attract consumers.

Eager entrepreneurs tried again during the dot-com boom, introducing a rash of simplified kitchen computers designed to get tech-wary users online fast. Known as Internet appliances, these computers had no hard drive yet cost as much as a full-fledged PC. The Netpliance iOpener, for example, was aimed at "50-year-olds and above and the female community"—groups seen as needing kinder, gentler, and tightly curtailed access to the web (it connected only to preselected websites). The iOpener sank faster than a half-baked meatloaf.

On the kitchen scene today, the "media fridge" keeps popping up on tech-watch blogs as a symbol of the smart kitchen. Promising to coordinate menu planning with television and web surfing, these hybrid white goods have had limited impact on consumers, although add-on electronic calendars and photo storage devices—virtual magnets for the kitchen's favorite bulletin board—have been more successful. When it comes to kitchen computing, however, most people simply hook up an ordinary computer or laptop.

The first theorists of the modern kitchen, Catharine Beecher (1800–1878) and Christine Frederick (1883–1970), copied the floor plans of ship galleys and factory floors in their drive to make kitchens more efficient. The first wave of electric appliances was marketed by utility companies to boost energy consumption. Various gadgets were designed to make cooking a meal more like making a car: tool-assisted, time-managed, and scientific. Progressive designers treated the kitchen as a tiny factory where things get made (meals, mainly). Toasters were advertised as aids to production, yet they served to accelerate consumption—of pre-sliced, factory-baked bread.

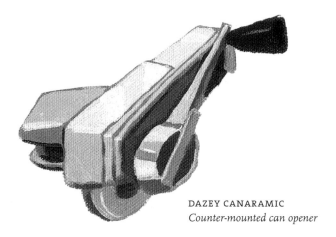

DAZEY CANARAMIC
Counter-mounted can opener

Another gadget tied to processed foods is the can opener. Morphing from modest handheld cranks into dramatic built-in devices, can openers went countertop in the 1930s and 40s, their mechanical guts hiding inside shapely shells inspired by trains and cars. In the 1950s a huge range of design and price options appealed to consumers hooked on tinned vegetables and tail fins.

Today, the kitchen has morphed from factory to information hub. In 2003, Whirlpool CEO Henry Marcy V called the kitchen "the command center of the home." This space age image has its roots in Whirlpool's "Miracle Kitchen," a demonstration project that toured the U.S. in 1957. At the center of the Miracle Kitchen was a planning area housing a telephone, audio-visual remote controls, and a closed-circuit TV monitor. Today, many kitchens include a computer and office niche in their floor plans. Pushing data, images, and brands has supplanted the production of things in the working lives of most middle-class American wage earners. As more and more meals exit their cartons and head straight for the microwave, today's digital tools zone the kitchen as a place to buy and serve branded goods and mass media. Meanwhile, cooking appliances are going back into hiding in upscale kitchens. Refrigerators masquerade as cabinetry, and "appliance garages" (complete with rolling garage doors) keep smaller machines out of sight, ready for use on ritual occasions, such as the Festival of the Waffle Iron, Midsummer Night's Popcorn, and the Ultra Slim Fest.

Too many gadgets clutter rather than clarify; the effort required to retrieve, operate, and clean small appliances often outbalances their promise of convenience. "Smart" systems that integrate audio, heating, lighting, and surveillance can be so challenging to use, their owners quickly abandon them. Behind the relative success and failure of

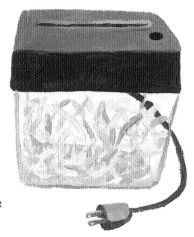

MINI PAPER SHREDDER
No bigger than a toaster

these engineered solutions to domestic tasks loom deeper questions about the computerized home. Media scholar David Morley argues that the soul of the smart house is not intelligence but rather security: both the emotional security of a place in which information and its mysterious machinery is personalized and domesticated, and physical security against the threat of crime, terror, and identity theft. In the contemporary kitchen, paper may be shredded more often than carrots or cheese. Yet, as upscale housing design continues to pursue the ideal of privacy at any cost, real privacy is increasingly undermined by ad ware, web crawling, and online shopping.

Meanwhile, the house itself is on the move, with cell phones and iPods becoming "mobile homes" that blow bubbles of ambient privacy around each consumer. The cell phone is the roller bag of communications: its portability and multiple functions allow users to drag their entire media suitcase with them when they leave the house while making them oblivious to the personal space of others. The "cell yell" is the barbaric "Yawp" of the mobile masses.

Technology's role in the home is not simply to process incoming information while keeping out real and virtual intruders. A really smart house is one that nurtures multiple intelligences: musical, artistic, mathematical, and culinary. Design tools are hibernating on hard drives and servers everywhere, in the form of fonts, image programs, video tools, and more. The home is not only a designed environment but also as an environment for design, whether it's creating a more beautiful meal or printing a fund-raising flyer.

My fridge is noisy, but it doesn't talk to me. We do have a computer in the kitchen, however. Everyone in the household uses it for art projects, homework help, and Internet research. Although we shop and pay bills on it, the computer in the kitchen is mainly used for work-

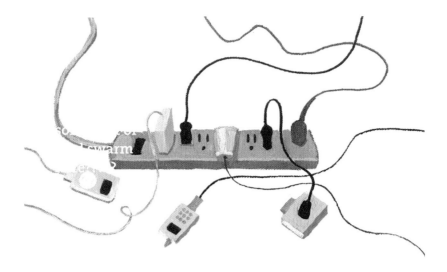

ing with words and images: drafting essays and reports, blogging and checking email, managing photos and doing design. I wrote this book with kids playing to my left and dinner simmering to my right.

Kitchen technology has long based its sale pitches on the freedom that the latest gizmo offers to female consumers. In one ad from the 1950s, a fashionably dressed lady on her way out the door declares, "My time's my own . . . my kitchen is Kelvinator!" Feminist historians, however, have noted that labor-saving devices helped raise standards of cleanliness and create new tasks. For example, the widespread embrace of automatic washing machines and dryers encouraged more frequent cleaning of sheets, towels, and pajamas and derailed the commercial out-of-home laundry business.

Not so with the computer in our kitchen. Far from escalating the housework, the downstairs laptop has helped me create pockets of independence and creativity inside the most active service sector of the house. Do you want a smart kitchen? Then stick microchips, web cams, and barcode readers inside your appliances. Do you want smart people? Then put the computer out in full view, where everyone can use it. Especially Mommy. **JL**

Bubble Trouble

Numerous web-only computers, designed for kitchen use, appeared during the peak of the Internet boom. Consumers never caught on, however, and most models were yanked off the market as the Internet chuck wagon began to crash.

AUDREY Introduced by 3com in 2000, the Audrey was quietly euthanized six months later. Operated with a digital pen and touch screen rather than a keyboard, Audrey was designed to conserve counter space and to attract the eye with her trendy, swoopy "blobject" curves.

EVILLA Equipped with a jaunty upright screen, SONY's eVilla came and went in 2001. Internet access was limited to websites created by SONY's business partners—no full-blown surfing allowed. Users couldn't load their own software onto the appliance, which had no hard drive.

GATEWAY/AOL INTERNET APPLIANCE
Introduced in 2000 and discontinued in 2001, this device wedded specific online content (AOL) with specific hardware (Gateway). It was a marriage that quickly came undone. The perky, Disney-esque curves weren't enough to warm consumers to this short-range appliance.

ICEBOX Launched in 2000, Salton's Icebox was a hub connecting a family of smart appliances, including a bread maker, coffeepot, and microwave. The hub could be placed anywhere in the home, so you could bake bread from your bedroom or make popcorn from the john. The model shown here (2004) is no longer available.

CONSCIOUS

CLUELESS

BAGGAGE CLAIMS

Exiting off an airport escalator one dark and weary midnight, I happened to trip over the enormous roller bag of a traveler just ahead of me. As he turned to glare at me for daring to bump his bag and violate his personal space, I discovered the answer to a question that had troubled me for some time: my irrational dislike of wheeled luggage.

I am one of the last people in the Western world to carry my luggage rather than pulling it behind me on wheels. Any visit to the airport or train station has become a tactical mission to avoid colliding with fleets of bags clattering along behind their generally clueless owners. Some intrepid travelers have not just one or but wheeled conveyances in tow—each with a pile of smaller parcels clinging on like baby chimp. Many are talking on their cell phones as well.

What's wrong with roller bags? Until that fateful night, I lacked any coherent rationale for disdaining this hugely popular and remarkably clever object. After all, roller bags prevent back injury while allowing people to bring along three seasons of clothing on an overnight trip. Why pack light when you can pack with wheels? Why lug your luggage when you can roll it instead?

The traveler in question (let's call him Roller Bob) was angry with *me* for not being aware of *his* suitcase. Yet Roller Bob was as oblivious of his own luggage as I was. The very appeal of roller bags lies in their ability to escape the attention of their users (and thus to transfer said awareness to the pedestrians all around them). Roller bags let people forget how much they're carrying—until someone trips over the hulking load behind them. Like iPods and BlackBerries, roller bags wrap their users in a cocoon of oblivion.

There's nothing wrong with roller bags per se. The object is perfectly brilliant, but when people use it, they slip into a state of mobile stupor. Good object; annoying behavior. Indeed, the roller bag is one of many handy gadgets that expand the reach of one's personal space, from cell phones and SUVs to umbrellas, hoop skirts, and extra-large sun hats. People who employ such conveyances can minimize their impact on those around them by staying alert to the extra space they and their objects occupy. **EL**

Burdens on Society

Alternative conveyances
for the
overloaded traveler

WIDE LOAD

RIDE-ON LUGGAGE

FREQUENT FLYER

Mobile Village

ROLLING FURNITURE Objects equipped with wheels are marvelously convenient—and potentially dangerous. Using your Aeron chair as a step ladder is frowned upon in even the most adventuresome workplace. The basic rolling library stool has a brilliantly simple interface: the rubber rim descends to lock the wheels when you stand on the stool. (Mobile step ladders use the same principle.) Clean the rubber rim occasionally to keep the brake functioning.

ROLLING BACKPACKS Parents today are compelled to buy roller backpacks for their kids to prevent stress injuries caused by the enormous pile of books they need to haul around each day. Perhaps the real issue here is too much homework. If kids weren't so overloaded with take-home duties, maybe they wouldn't need to drive their books to the bus stop.

ROLLING CHILDREN Children are not yet bred with built-in wheels (or brakes), but they clamor for mobility just like the rest of us. Heely shoes, which faithfully appear under countless holiday trees each year, offer a high-speed enhancement for the slow child. Unfortunately, these shoes work best indoors, where 100-meter stretches of unobstructed flooring are tough to come by. Thus children on wheels are often sighted at malls and airports shortly after Christmas. Caution: your kid might get run over by a suitcase.

ROLLING WATER TANK While people in developed nations are eagerly attaching wheels to every conceivable object, rolling conveyances of any kind are in short supply in many parts of the world. In rural Africa, countless people live long distances from clean water. The Q Drum, designed by P. J. and J. P. S. Hendrikse in South Africa in 1993, is both a container and a simple wheel. (If you think your overnight bag is too heavy to lift, try carrying seventy-five liters of water two miles home to your family.)

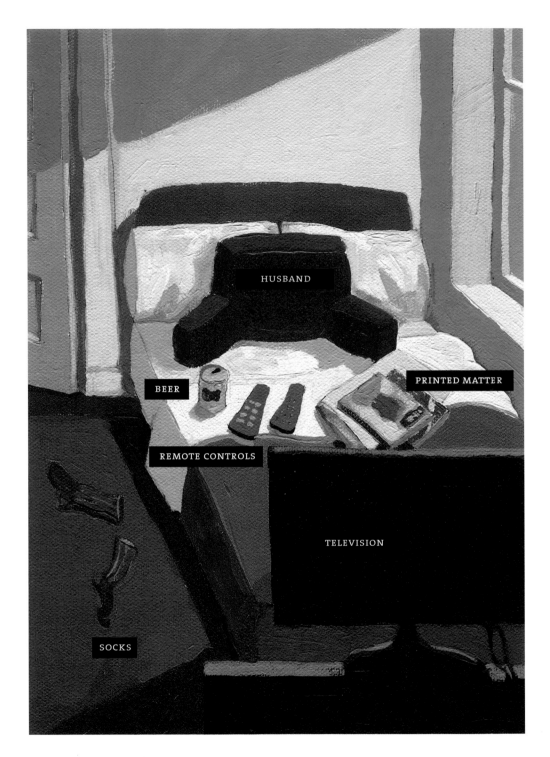

HABITAT OF THE ADULT MALE

BEDTIME READINGS

Some years ago, I attended a staff luncheon for a colleague who had recently adopted a beautiful baby girl from China. This single woman had courageously decided to build a family on her own. Home together with her daughter for a few weeks, she was proud, happy, and tired. Her eyes were red, her back hurt, and she wasn't sleeping much.

"What you need is a husband," announced another mom sitting at our table.

Silence fell around us like a heavy diaper.

"What I mean," this married mother quickly explained, "is one of those corduroy pillows with little arms on the side, that let you read a book or hold your baby in bed."

Indeed, *everyone* needs a husband, and I would even have one myself if they weren't so awful to look at. Pillows have become an essential comfort in the bedroom (and in other places you might nod off, from airplanes to business meetings). In some cultures, objects designed to elevate the head during sleep are works of art of the highest order; in others, they are plumped and patterned symbols of material comfort. Throw pillows are both decorative and functional, serving to customize furniture by fitting around individual bodies. I've talked with small-stature adults who use pillows to adjust the "fit" of over-scale sofas to suit their personal scale.

In designing your own bed, you will want to consider issues of function, comfort, and message as well as fabrics and color schemes. One pillow may be all you need to sleep with; indeed, some people travel everywhere with their favorite pillow, strapping it to their roller bags or heading out into the wilderness with this one irreplaceable life partner stuffed into their backpacks. Beds aren't just for sleeping; additional pillows are needed for reading, eating, mating, watching TV, and participating in conference calls. Choosing pillows is a momentous endeavor. How many pillows, and how big? Ruffled or rectilinear? Feathers or foam? Square, oblong, or shaped like a giant hot dog? What will your pillows say to you each night when you climb into bed with them? And how will you feel about them in the morning? EL

Pillows and the Reign of Function

Pillows are more than just status objects; they are ergonomic equipment designed to support the body at rest, work, and play.

These functional classics need nothing more than a fashion update to become must-have objects for the well-dressed bed.

THE HUSBAND This classic piece of portable furniture is like having an easy chair in your bed. The standard husband is now available with handy pockets as well as high-tech conveniences such as heaters and vibrators. What more could a wife want—except, perhaps a dog?

THE WEDGE If you get bored with your husband, try the wedge, designed to elevate the pelvis during lovemaking. According to theory, the wedge provides an ideal angle of penetration. Some users just think it's naughty to present their privates on a ramp. Whatever its source of charm, this functional object does pose decorating challenges.

THE WIFE

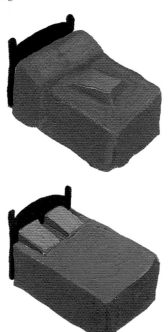

THE DOG

CONGO NECK REST Pillows don't have to be soft. The neck rest above was created by the Luba people, who live in the present-day Democratic Republic of Congo. Measuring a little over six inches in height, this tiny sculpture was carved in the nineteenth century and served to elevate the head during sleep. In addition to providing comfort, the object protected the impressive hair style of its user, whose tresses required around fifty hours to arrange into wedge-like forms. (Collection of the Metropolitan Museum of Art, accession number 1981.399.)

TRAVEL NECKREST These moon-shaped bags of buckwheat may be unsightly, but less so than your slack-mouthed head bobbing up and down in economy class. When you must sleep in a fully upright position, a travel neckrest provides a trace of comfort and a scrap of dignity. Try wearing one to your next leadership retreat or prayer breakfast.

ELIZABETHAN
NECKREST

HAVE A NICE HAIR DAY

CROISSANT
NECKREST

NECKREST
W/SPRINKLES

How to Make Your Bed

DREAD SPREAD To achieve this dowdy look, arrange two pillows at the head of the bed like a pair of flat, matronly breasts. Tuck a bedspread (tufted chenille or quilted poly) snugly under the bust line.

THE WEDDING CAKE Decorating professionals call this style the wedding cake: a tiered stack of pillows lying flat on the bed in ascending size. The tiniest pillow sits, like a prize, on the very top. Bride and groom sold separately.

FILE DRAWER A bed can accommodate a vast number of pillows stacked parallel to the headboard. It is not uncommon for the pillows to take up more room than the people. Arrange from large to small. Have fun with contrasting colors, textures, and patterns. Have fun throwing your pillows on the floor each night and putting them back in the correct order each morning.

YOU TUBE In place of feminine puffery and frou frou, some homesteaders crave the crisp geometry of one long cylinder.

THE EXISTENTIALIST
Perhaps making one's bed each day is a false symbol of order and a pointless waste of time. After all, last night's bedding is not truly fresh just because you've smoothed it out and tucked it under.

THE MCMATTRESS Massive houses require massive furniture. McMansion-scale beds have extra-thick mattresses that require special sheets, spreads, and skirts.

THE POET Many people use the space beneath their beds as an extra closet. The entire bed can even become a storage device. Books and papers covered the bed of poet W. H. Auden, who is remembered for both his brilliant verse and his slovenly apartment.

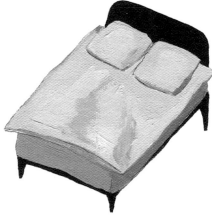

THE SPARTAN The simple duvet cover lends itself to frequent laundering and easy bed making.

STILL LIFE WITH PRICE TAG

RAISING THE HONOR BAR

In the modern American hotel room, visitors are treated in turn as respected guests and potential thieves. Words such as "convenience," "honor," and "courtesy" politely delineate a curious code of ethics. If I spent the night at your home, you might not find it necessary to point out that I shouldn't leave with your bathrobe. But in hotel rooms, where miniature sewing kits and tiny bars of soap are compliments of the house, you will often see a tag like this one:

This bathrobe is provided for your **CONVENIENCE.** *If you would like to take it home, we would be happy to bill you*

$80

Bottled water is the most frequently purchased in-room amenity. But what about the little fridge stocked with candy, booze, and soda pop? It is called an "honor bar" because it would be dishonorable to replace its contents with identical items purchased for a fraction of the price at the corner deli.

Many hotels in the U.S. have started showing interest in ecology. A sign like this may appear beside your pillow:

Help us save the earth.
Each year, countless gallons of water and
detergent are consumed washing sheets
and towels that have hardly been used.
We will change the bed sheets in this room
every third day during your stay.
If you wish to have fresh linens sooner,
please place this card on the bed.

Most people don't launder their sheets every day at home. (Just keeping the bed made is effort enough.) But the difference at home is that when *you* conserve resources, *you* get to keep the money. Those save-the-planet cards in hotels are motivated by economics; it costs a lot of money to wash all of the sheets and towels every day. Hotels have caught on to the idea that ecology can make good business sense, or what's called "market-based environmentalism." So why not be honest about the economics? How about this?

Our hotel is conserving resources
and keeping costs down by laundering
the sheets every third day.
If you'd like your sheets changed more
often, please place this card on the bed.

Or this:

Spilled your drink? Wet the bed?
Had sex? Got your period?
We'd be happy to change the sheets,
but it will cost you
$10

The green-onomics of American hotels would be more credible if these establishments were doing more to conserve resources elsewhere. Novel ideas employed in Europe include windows that actually open (in lieu of mandatory air-conditioning), hallway lights equipped with motion sensors (instead of blasting every public area 24/7 with incandescent floods), and large-scale shampoo dispensers in the shower.

Another clever concept at work in many European hotels is a light switch activated by the guest's electronic room key. Slide the card in and the lights go on; remove the card, and they all shut off. This ingenious system forces guests to turn out the lights when they leave the room; furthermore, the lights automatically return to the configuration you last left them in. Ideas like this one don't require any phony signage. They just work. **EL**

AIN'T NO MOUNTAIN HIGH ENOUGH *Although breasts naturally gravitate towards sea level, contemporary bra design seeks ever more astonishing altitudes. Shortness of breath is not uncommon.*

UNDERWEAR ARCHITECTURE

On New York City's Upper East Side there is a fancy lingerie shop with a big poster in the window explaining that most women are wearing the wrong bra. "Come inside," the sign beckons, "for a professional fitting." Why? The wrong bra could damage your breasts. The wrong bra could make you look ten years older. The wrong bra could lower your credit rating.

With so much at stake, one day I finally entered. Racks of silky merchandise filled the small store, and mysterious banks of closed drawers lined the walls. Visitors can shop the open rack for hand-crafted teddies and tiny thongs, but to really experience the place, one must be fitted by an expert with access to what's in those drawers.

To do this requires an appointment. An appointment? Had I known I'd need an appointment, I would have gone ahead and sched-uled surgery at the Park Avenue Implant Spa down the block. But I had made it this far, and I was determined to complete my mission.

Ahead of me were two authentic neighborhood socialites; they had called ahead and would be seen immediately. A less fortunate customer, a woman about sixty-five with an enormous mono-bosom, was turned away in disgrace. "I'm looking for a G-cup," she said. "No, no," said the ruthless gatekeeper. "We don't carry that sort of thing."

I, blessed with an utterly average body, was told to come back in an hour, which I did, clinging fast to my appointment, and to my hope. On duty was Maria, a well-dressed, middle-aged woman with a Caribbean accent, who led me down a passageway lined with grim X-ray diagrams of women wearing ill-fitting bras. She unlocked a cu-bicle and followed me inside, shutting the latch with a decisive click.

"Strip from the waist up," she said.

I rarely get naked even for my husband, preferring to soften reality with dim lights, a silky camisole, and a glass of wine. But here I was, half-naked and fully sober, standing in front of a perfect stranger, displaying my less-than-perfect breasts under surgical-grade fluorescents. What next? Would she take my pulse? Shave my head?

Maria didn't touch me at all. She studied me solemnly and ordered me to turn around a few times. After about forty seconds of deliberation, she pronounced, "32C." For a dozen years, I had been wearing size 34B, purchased in a hurry at Target or Vickie's Secret. It turns out that the cup was too small and the back measurement was too big—and that this is women's single most common fitting error. Maria could tell exactly what I needed without a tape measure. The cup, I learned, gives shape to the breasts, while the band does most of the work of supporting their weight.

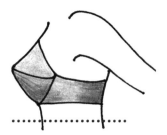

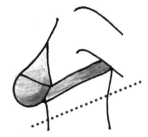

BAND IS HORIZONTAL,
SUPPORTING BREASTS

BAND IS TOO LONG AND
RIDES UP IN BACK

Maria returned to the cubicle with an armful of bras. She watched as I tried them on, instructing me to push and prod my flesh correctly into the molded carapace of each garment. (Everything goes in there, even the fat blobs under your arms.) Most of the foam-padded constructions Maria brought back from hidden storage fit pretty well. She seemed to know each make and model inside out—essential knowledge in her line of work, because the lingerie industry has established no common standards regarding bra construction. Determining the right size is just the beginning of a proper fit, as each manufacturer interprets the numbers its own way

I left the fancy bra shop with $300 worth of high-tech engineering. Contrary to popular belief, wearing a bra won't prevent your breasts from sagging. A well-fitted bra will, however, provide a more youthful profile (if you want one), and it is more comfortable than a bra that is too tight, too big, or bears too much weight from the shoulders. Yet even a carefully chosen bra will fall short of perfection. Why? Bras are completely symmetrical; breasts aren't. Bras stay the same size all month; breasts don't. Perhaps some future brassiere specialist will invent a self-cleaning, auto-adjusting, custom-fitting bra. And perhaps it's already here—your own skin, if you can accept the shape it naturally wants to take. **E L**

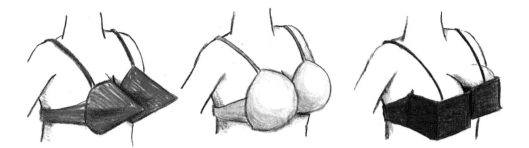

BAUHAUS BRAS Bras were invented to reshape the female breast. What the ideal shape might be is a matter of fashion and personal taste. Over the years, bras have assumed the profiles of bullets, rocket ships, ice cream cones, hamburger buns, and other objects. The designs proposed here are a tribute to the great Bauhaus artist Oscar Schlemmer, whose wondrous theater costumes employed geometric solids and machine parts. Complete the look with aluminum panties.

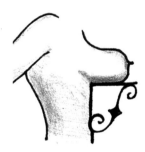

SHELF BRA Bras create a rigid architecture for the liquid female bosom. Shelf bras or "balconettes" push the breast up as far as possible from below, while concealing as little flesh as possible.

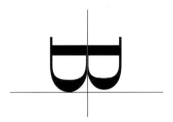

B-CUP B is for breasts, boobs, and Bodoni. As in a natural bosom, the bulges in the letter B don't match exactly.

MICRO FASHION Tired of over-structured undergarments? Make your own minimal lingerie with just a few lengths of ribbon.

BRA *Cut one length of ribbon for the chest band; cut two pieces for straps. Tie together.*

THONG *Cut one length of ribbon for waist. Cut a second length for crotch. Tie together.*

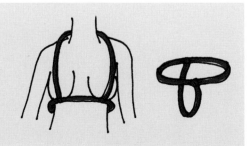

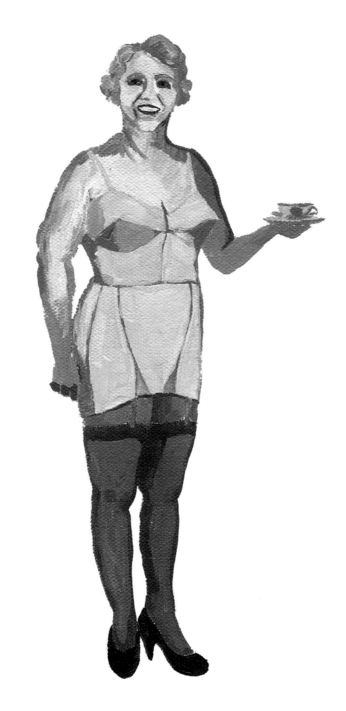

NICE LADY; SCARY UNDERWEAR

Design and the Elastic Waistband

When I was growing up, my maternal grandmother always wore a girdle—a horrid rubbery thing with as many gills and gussets as a primeval shark. A respectable woman of her generation, no matter how slim, wouldn't leave home or receive company without wearing a full armor of compression undergarments. (Furthermore, in the days before panty hose, a woman needed a girdle to hold her stockings up.) The baby boomers overthrew such restrictive mores, burning their bras and forsaking their girdles. My hip, sexy, forever-young mother never wore a girdle, and never, ever would I.

Or so I thought as a child. Today, a new generation of body-shapers are being marketed to style-conscious women of every age. Men are wearing girdles, too—they call them "body shirts," "compression tanks," and "support boxers." Millennial girdles use heavy-duty Lycra instead of straps and belts to erase panty lines and firm up jiggle zones. The Spanx line of undergear, whose product styles include "power panty" and "slim cognito," speaks squarely to the chick lit set. These flesh-bruising modern garments offer various degrees of coverage; conflict erupts where Lycra meets unbridled flab. **EL**

THE	THE	THE	THE
MUFFIN TOP	SQUID	PORK SAUSAGE	WHOLE ENCHILADA

MESSY
SITUATIONS

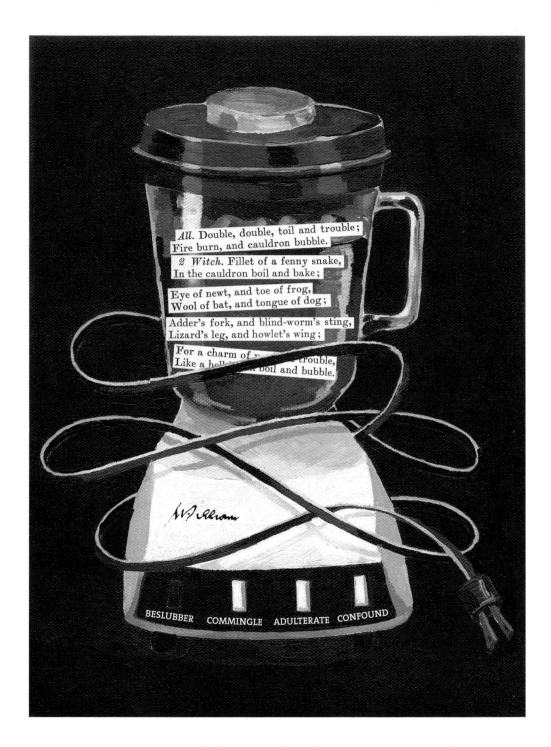

MACBETH BLENDER *Shakespeare is credited with introducing 3,000 new words into written English. "Osterize" wasn't one of them.*

HOW OBJECTS EXPLAIN THEMSELVES

One child is making a smoothie. "Mommy, what am I supposed to do? Grate, grind, stir, puree, whip, mix, or blend it?" She is operating an Osterizer 10-speed blender. Behind those words loom unique destinies for chosen foods: the pureed potato, the ground nut, the whipped cream. To the child, however, this thesaurus of mechanical mastication is simply confusing. After all, she doesn't know that those little push buttons can only deliver different speeds. That their mysteries are chimerical. That all they can really offer is degrees of mush.

Meanwhile, another child is baking a cake. He dumps his ingredients into the handsome bowl of a KitchenAid standing mixer. The cake box directs him to mix on low until blended, and then mix on medium for two minutes. No problem. The KitchenAid mixer, adapted for home use by Egmont Ahrens in 1936, still sports a simple sliding knob that slots into ten numbers distributed across its long bulbous hood. The numbers clearly describe a continuum of speeds. A click lets you know that you have advanced to a new speed.

In *The Design of Everyday Things*, Donald Norman argues that a thoughtful and effective object uses visual cues to explain to the user how it works. A well-designed object diagrams its own operation. And it thanks you when you've performed the task correctly. (Designers call those little clicks of confirmation "feedback.") The KitchenAid control is an example of a "natural mapping" of the machine's controls onto its functioning: the sliding of the knob increases the speed of the motor, and the numbers translate quantity into speed. You can almost see the sliding metal slat interacting with the motor. (This feature is called "visibility.") The chattier Osterizer works, too—any adult user understands that the buttons map a continuum—but the manufacturers needlessly detracted from the universality of the design by replacing numbers with words. Compare microwave ovens with buttons marked POPCORN and BAKED POTATO. Why not controls for more exotic or upscale foodstuffs, such as EYE OF NEWT and TOE OF FROG?

At the heart of Norman's account of human-centered design are the twin ideas of affordances and constraints. Affordances are those properties of a thing that determine how it might be used—whether it's the pouring of water from a spout, the throwing of a ball, or the turning of a door latch. Designers use such features as shape, color, position, and texture communicate the intended uses of the object. A ceramic mug is designed to be lifted by its handle, protecting the drinker from the heat of the cup. The handle also affords hanging on a hook, and some aficionados might choose to wrap their tea bag around it. If the loop of the handle were too tight for comfort, or too large for a sense of security, or located on the bottom of the cup, or made out of cloth, it would no longer invite these actions.

The ten raised rectangles on the front of the Osterizer afford pushing. Everything about them, from their diminutive size and up-front placement to the slight indentations that dimple their tiny tops—communicate their function as buttons. So too, the KitchenAid's round, firm, black knob, a handy finial abutting the end of a slim slat of steel, clearly affords sliding. In both cases, design has been used to render more visible and more tactile the machines' proper operation.

But speed brings danger. Might not a finger be CHOPPED, nerves GRATED, or a marriage PULVERIZED? Product designers marshal constraints in order to limit affordances. The first three buttons of the Osterizer are red. They must be held down in order to keep the motor on. This constraint prevents over-mixing and limits the fruit and ice storm released when small children or adults seeking margaritas use the blender without securing its lid. Sliding the KitchenAid's handy knob meets a certain resistance—one cannot speed the machine up quickly, reducing the risk of flour tornados and spoon loss. Its rotary blade is sunk deep within the bowl, constraining fingers from merging with the machine.

Affordances entered the vocabulary of designers from ecology. In 1977, James Gibson defined affordances as qualities of the environment that support certain actions. Thus a firm, flat ground affords walking, a tree branch affords clinging, and a cave affords shelter— whether or not such actions actually take place. (Mars might afford the growing of asparagus—but that fact would by no means indicate that asparagus is native to it.) "An affordance," Gibson writes, "is not bestowed upon an object by the need of an observer and by his act of perceiving it. The object offers what it does because of what it is."

Affordances can help us understand the genius and stupidity of everyday objects such as blenders and mixers. But affordances, derived from the science of ecology as well as the world of product design, can also illuminate the environments of daily life. Take flatness, which Gibson identifies as one of the most important features promoting the development of terrestrial life. Firm, extended surfaces afford locomotion and thus enable many forms of animal behavior, including equilibrium, standing, lying, manipulation, and even aspects of visual perception.

Flatness also affords architecture. Many houses are built on flat or flattened land; hillside houses must insert conditions of flatness into steep terrain in order to take advantage of other affordances such as protection from intruders or the cooling and warming properties of earth. Floors support standing, walking, lying, and the storing of furniture, while stairs create a series of flat planes in order to cope with level change. Tables support dishes, glasses, computers, and the morning newspaper. Beds are soft tables that afford lying-down.

But flatness, like GRIND and LIQUEFY, poses risks to household order. At my house, the flat expanse of the floor also affords the heaping of wet towels, dirty laundry, and abandoned socks. Meanwhile, the lovely raised flatness of tables, desks, and counters affords the accumulation of books, papers, half-filled wine bottles, and last week's mail. Beds collect unfolded laundry, unwanted pillows, random remote controls, and the occasional amorous head louse. (Natural terrains, writes Gibson, are also "cluttered," a word he uses to describe the challenge posed by swamps, brinks, slopes, and crevices in the flatlands of locomotion.)

At my house, flatness, like free time, clean laundry, and the gas tax, is both curse and blessing. Flatness affords our feasting, our conversations, our writing, and our slumber. Yet flatness is elusive: no sooner cleared of clutter, precious flatlands seem almost instantly to amass topographic complexity. Yet it is neither the imbecility of children nor the harried habits of a working mother that causes this accumulation. It is because flatness affords its own destruction. **JL**

Conserving Domestic Flatlands

Is it possible to constrain the affordances of flatness—to keep flatness open for physical use and visual order?

CLUTTER MAGNET One dirty cup quickly attracts bad company. Cheryl Mendelson, law professor turned housekeeping expert, applies the "broken window theory" from neighborhood policing to household management. If a broken window goes unfixed in a neighborhood, more serious signs of neglect and crime are likely to gather around it. So too, a dish or newspaper left on the kitchen table will quickly gather mail, keys, phones, and other modern debris all around it. Vigilance with the first signs of clutter can prevent a mass riot.

ACTS AND MONUMENTS Center a special vase, decorative bowl, or household god on an end table, side table, or shelf. By strategically occupying the flat area, a well-placed *objet* has the power to ward off the piling up of mere objects.

LID LORE The lid of this translucent plastic clothes hamper keeps the bin looking tidy, while the half-round cuts provide both a handle and a ventilation.

Alas, the neat lid begets sloppy behavior; some family members would rather throw soiled items at the bin than lift off the lid and place them inside.

The lid enables the bin to double as a handy snack table or laptop station. The lid's unintended extra functions could outweigh the bad behavior it encourages.

Toy Management Manifesto

1. 99 percent of the stuff you buy for your kids is junk, destined to be forgotten within a few days. Yes, even wooden blocks from Germany and baby dolls that spew bodily fluids.

2. The phrase "hours of fun" is an empty promise.

3. You can't put stuff away if there's no place to put it.

4. Storage bins for toys should be cheap, plentiful, and open.

5. It is always easier to get a toy out than to put it away.

6. It is also easier to toss the toy into an open box than to pry off a lid before you do so.

7. Throwing the toy in the trash is even easier.

8. The law of entropy holds for toys just as it holds for the universe: all things gradually descend into disorder. Only, toys descend faster.

9. As things lose order, they lose value. A thousand Legos are a world of possibilities. A single Lego is totally worthless.

10. Better to have many small bins to organize specific categories (Sharpies, rubber snakes, fake food) than a few large bins where civilizations clash (lacrosse sticks, model cars, random chess pieces).

OPEN SOURCE This plastic bin costs under two dollars. It can stack or nest, and it has no lid. It's small enough for a kid to carry, and big enough to hold a dozen Barbies and all their swag.

SEALED SHUT This cloth-covered box with a fitted lid looks lovely (especially in artfully staged catalog photos). Alas, the effort of lifting the lid inhibits use, while the high cost inhibits buying enough boxes to actually organize your stuff.

Writing on Toilet Paper

Have you ever lived in a household where everyone seemed to avoid putting a fresh roll of toilet paper on the holder when the old one had run out? For days, even weeks, the dispenser would display a naked cardboard tube while the fresh roll sat on the floor or on top of the toilet tank. You can blame your roommates for being lazy boobs, or you can look at how the design of the paper holder itself may have encouraged the rude behavior.

Design has psychological as well as mechanical functions. An ordinary toilet paper holder can instill feelings of security, freedom, and restraint in addition to keeping the clean roll off the dirty floor. We are toilet paper "users" not only when sitting on the porcelain throne but also when taking on the role of homemaker, housekeeper, janitor, and aspiring toilet-paper thief. Design speaks to various needs and desires while it heeds (or hinders) our actions. **EL**

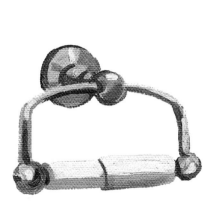

SPRING LOADED This type of device requires a complex series of dual-handed actions in order to free the depleted roll and insert a new one. (We counted six distinct hand movements, some demanding significant dexterity and at least a high school education.) Despite the inconvenience, people remain attracted to designs like this one because they keep the paper firmly locked in place once it is put there, providing a comforting sense of toilet-paper security.

OPEN ENDED Various designs are available that hold the paper on a simple bracket with no locking mechanism. All that's needed to constrain the roll from leaping off the wall and spinning away into the great unknown is an upturned angle or a finial that's a little bigger than the main bar but small enough to pass through the gut of the cardboard core. Changing rolls is now a one-handed task requiring just a few motions.

LOCK DOWN In public restrooms, rolls of paper often are literally under lock and key. Why? To deter toilet paper theft, a real and present danger in contemporary society. Many models also appear designed to deter excessive paper use by inhibiting the flow of material out of the unit. Pity she who sits on the pot next to one of those giant wheels of toilet paper that has been just squeezed into the locked dispenser. While she's in the stall, she might study the archeology of discarded dispenser design. Holes, paint lines, or the abandoned shells of dispensers past are often a sign that a new cleaning company has retooled the joint in order to standardize all its sites.

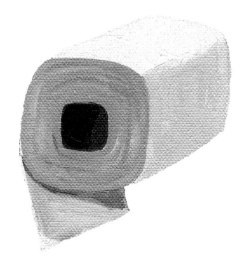

SQUARE DEAL The first toilet paper dispensers were books. With the rise of printing in the Renaissance, literate folks began ripping a few pages from a cheap tome or pamphlet for personal hygiene purposes. Commercial toilet paper has been marketed since the 1880s. Shown here is an experimental design by architect Shigeru Ban; the toilet paper is wrapped around a core with a square profile rather than a round one. (Shigeru Ban is famous for creating entire buildings out of cardboard tubes.) His roll dispenses paper only with resistance, bumping along as the user pulls on it rather than unfurling smoothly. The roll itself, rather than the dispenser, inhibits use. Created for the exhibition "Re-Design: Daily Products of the 21st Century," produced by Kenya Hara, 2000.

MUDDY WATERS *Piles of paper are a mirror of your mental landscape.*

PILES: EVERYONE GETS THEM

Piles are a common source of misery. At home and at work, mountains of paper—bills, letters, memos from school, postcards from your local litigator—accumulate unchecked on any flat surface. The paperless future predicted for decades by technophiles remains as mythic as wireless communication and fat-free cheesecake. My home office is the messiest part of a more or less orderly house. Here I sit surrounded by piles. Although I use the computer all day, I am awash with paper: galleys to correct, reports to read and respond to, tickets and itineraries for future travel, a postcard for an exhibition I want to see, notes for a book I hope to write, and more, much more.

I could file these items away in a drawer, but then they would be forgotten. Productivity experts suggest that only finished business should be banished to a file cabinet. Active projects need to stay in view to stay on track, so unless your desk is the size of a regulation tennis court, some of your paper is going to end up in piles.

A stack of stuff can harbor secret intelligence A certain red folder, say, protruding jauntily from a dreary heap of clippings and computer printouts could flag a crucial point in time, signaling a mental order that would catastrophically collapse should the pile get sorted by a clueless spouse or zealous co-worker. Some people defend their piles as the key to their creativity; nonetheless, those same defenders (myself included) often feel a crushing sense of dismay, inertia, and even shame when confronted with masses of their own paper.

The old adage goes, "Out of sight, out of mind." Web designers talk about the need to "surface" information on the main page of a site, enticing users to go deeper without making them dig or search. Yet a home page can't present the complete content of everything a visitor might want to see; thus to save real estate, designers use bits and pieces to draw readers down to the next level. Likewise, an intelligent pile needs to show itself, providing ways into the stack. Dotting the edges of your computer screen with Post-it reminders is an instinctive form of surfacing. A bulletin board is a wall-mounted pile, employed to spatialize all manner of visual ephemera that might otherwise disappear from view.

Yet even those things that get pushed to the surface can escape from consciousness. That picture of your kids taken at summer camp five years ago may no longer attract your loving gaze, having faded into the proverbial woodwork. Tucked inside the urgent to-do folder sitting on your desk or kitchen counter are some actionables so past due, it's pointless to even bother with them now. (The angry letter you vowed to write after a crappy hotel stay in 2002? Forget about it.) Weeding your piles could make you feel better about all the stuff you *don't* have to do.

Just as the holiday shopping season winds down each year, the mail-order catalogs come flowing in from companies selling containers, boxes, shelving units, and closet systems so elaborate you could use them to open your own retail outlet. Having bought (and received) too much stuff over the holidays, some of us feel inspired to clean up for the new year and organize it all, for good. It's hard to make your own working spaces look like the ones in the magazines and catalogs, however, and maybe you shouldn't. People use numerous techniques to manage their piles, keeping their content within reach without getting buried alive. The key to designing a successful system lies in making it not just the transient result of a one-day cleaning frenzy but a pattern you can live with. **EL**

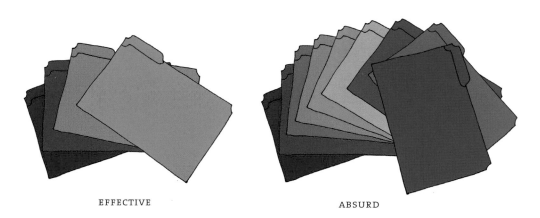

EFFECTIVE   ABSURD

COLOR CODING If your work lends itself to tidy categories, color-coded folders or labels can help you quickly find a particular file, providing a visual memory aid. Keep the categories few and simple, however, or the task of implementing the system (and remembering how it works) will outweigh the benefits of using it.

Pile Management

PAPER FOLDERS Standard office folders are designed for use inside the dark, closed drawers of file cabinets, but they also turn up in many productive piles. The act of sorting a pile into folders prompts you to throw away much of what you don't need.

TRANSPARENT SLEEVES Opaque paper folders have to be labeled (which takes time), and you can't tell what's inside of them without reading the labels (which takes more time). Transparent folders reveal their own contents and often don't need labels at all. Clear plastic sleeves are great for organizing small projects.

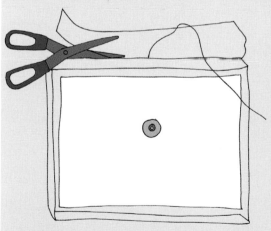

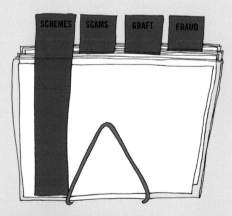

PLASTIC PORTFOLIOS For bigger projects, try clear plastic portfolios, the kind that close with a string that wraps around a button. I prefer to cut off the flap and string to make it easier to get papers in and out. Since the portfolio sits on my desk and travels around in my bag, it doesn't need to be sealed tighter than Tut's tomb—when a system is easy to use, you are more likely to use it.

STRIP LABELS Folders organized in a desktop file rack become a kind of vertical pile. Strips of paper sticking up out each file make it easy to find what's inside. When a folder needs to travel, just rotate the strip ninety degrees so it fits inside. Unlike stick-on labels, this quick method doesn't damage the folders, which can be endlessly recycled.

Ellen Lupton's Office

A person with two jobs, two kids, and a hyperactive publishing practice can't be expected to have a tidy desk. My home office is a humming, buzzing nest of frenetic production. Despite the real and apparent mess, I do crank out a lot of projects here while managing to keep the rest of my house reasonably neat. I can't claim that all the disorder improves my efficiency or state of mind. I always feel better after I take off a few hours to purge the old books and papers that I'm not using anymore. But I've come to accept that a certain level of disorder helps me keep things moving. I've found ways to fine-tune the clutter to support, rather than overwhelm, my day-to-day work life.

1. OPEN FILES Active folders are stored in wire racks. Strips of orange paper provide a highly visible and easy-to-maintain labeling system. A generous supply of extra folders and paper strips are kept at the front of the rack.

2. THE LOOSE STUFF Not everything deserves to be filed at all. Items needing immediate or ongoing attention sit right out on the desk. Eventually, it gets filed or thrown away.

3. BOXES AND BINS Some projects require more substantial piles. Open boxes cluster on the floor around my desk, harboring books, magazines, and thick wads of research.

4. RECYCLING You shouldn't have to get off your ass to get rid of unwanted paper. Keep an office-sized recycling bin within arm's reach.

5. BIG DESK Many desks are really just rinky-dink tables, wit no drawers or storage. My massive mother ship, which is over thirty-six inches deep, has huge drawers for storing files and supplies. Magnets stick to the powder-coated steel body, providing yet another way to pile. Made by Steel Case in the 1960s, the desk was purchased for a song from a scratch-and-dent furniture store.

6. BIG SCREEN A big screen (like a big desk) improves efficiency, allowing multiple files to be active and visible simultaneously. (A group of open windows is a kind of digital pile.)

7. CAFFEINE Preferred delivery mechanism: tea.

8. CORDS What a mess. But for me, it's better to have the cords out and exposed than to have to go hunting for them. For example, I keep a USB cord for my digital camera plugged in to my computer hub so that it's always there when I need to download photos.

9. PEN MOUSE A digital pen and tablet instead of a standard mouse is great for drawing, and it seems to lessen the wrist pain acquired from long days of clicking and dragging. Yes, the tablet has a cord. Yes, I'm left-handed. And yes, I keep a normal mouse on the right side, too, so my kids, husband, and other guests don't panic when they use my computer.

10. EAMES CHAIR I have always lacked the skill and inclination to use an adjustable ergonomic chair. This vintage Eames chair, padded with beige vinyl, offers hours of basic comfort.

11. PORTABLE HARD DRIVE I keep all my active projects on a portable hard drive, which allows me to carry my work with me when I travel or go to meetings without having to transfer files to and from my laptop. A portable drive also makes frequent backups less odious.

12. FLOOR PILE The floor space right next to my chair is an ideal spot to stage small piles that need to go with me to a meeting or presentation.

Al Gore's Office

No one ever got a Nobel prize for having an office that looks like New Year's Eve at the Container Store. Al Gore's work space provides a window into the busy, connected mind of someone with lots to do, lots to read, and lots to remember. Your personal work environment is an externalization of your brain, a physical repository for your current thinking and your living knowledge. Books, papers, and files keep information more or less visible so that you don't have to stuff it all inside your skull.

1. THE GREAT PLAIN OF PILES The surface of an executive-sized desk in the center of the room has been colonized entirely by piles. Enough knowledge is stored here to occupy a normal person for a lifetime.

2. SATELLITE DESK, WITH SATELLITE PILES A secondary desk is where the real action happens in this office. The work surface is small, but it's big enough to harbor numerous tiny piles.

3. MORE PILES Shelves provide another welcome home for piles. Some pilers use shelves to stack and sort priority projects in a linear way. For other pilers, the shelf is merely a graveyard, a place for stashing piles whose memory must be honored but who have scant chance for a second life.

4. MULTIPLE COMPUTER SCREENS A big computer screen enhances productivy; three huge screens are even better.

5. TELEVISION Most people don't try to work with the television turned on, but if you had your own station, like Al Gore's Current TV, you just might be tempted.

6. MOTIVATIONAL ART Everyone deserves to have some artwork in his or her office. Al Gore has a sculpture of a tree frog climbing up his wall. This is better than a "Hang in There" poster, but you can probably do better.

7. BRAINSTORM PAD Did you ever wonder what happens to those giant pads of paper that get hauled out on easels at town hall meetings and mandatory training sessions? Here's your answer: Al Gore takes them home and uses them to save the world.

8. ERGONOMIC CHAIR Advanced degree required.

TRIPTYCH WORKSTATION
DEVISED BY MARY CZERWINSKI

THE ART OF DISTRACTION Many people are forced to work on multiple projects simultaneously while under constant email alert (that alluring ping). Mary Czerwinski, a scientist employed by Microsoft, has observed how people function in this climate of constant interruption. Using custom spyware to study the behavior of some Microserf volunteers, she learned that they kept an average of eight windows open at a time and spent about twenty seconds looking at each one before flipping to another. Many workers had installed multiple computer screens on their desks so that they could keep more windows visible at once. When Czerwinski gave workers a giant 42-inch monitor, they completed tasks between 10 and 44 percent faster than workers supplied with a meager 15-inch monitor. Being able to glance from window to window proved advantageous.

MULTITASKING *Product designer Ron Gilad created this chandelier out of standard task lights. Called "Dear Ingo" in tribute to Ingo Maurer, the grand master of contemporary lighting design, Gilad's lamp is a commentary on our over-tasked existence.*

THE LURE OF MULTITASKING

6:00 p.m., California time. I'm chopping garlic and waiting for pasta water to boil. I am also advising a student, cordless phone tucked between my chin and shoulder in what is becoming the half-cocked, half-cooked posture of the pre-dinner hour. One child comes in search of cookies. Another can't find her shoes. (The first gets fed, the second shod.) Meanwhile, email keeps flowing into the nearby computer, as regular as the rising tides of the melting polar caps.

I always thought this was multitasking—the miraculous, super-human ability to do several things at once and do them all pretty well. This state of productive alert is increasingly expected of middle managers and working parents. Developing the multitasking metaphor, CEOs and WSDs (women seeking dignity) like to call the kitchen the "command center" of the contemporary home. Just as your PC processes several tasks simultaneously, the modern homemaker tries to meet multiple obligations at the same time using digital tools ranging from the microwave oven and the electric toaster to the cordless phone and the kitchen computer.

My kitchen, however, is no command center (implying safety from numbers)—it's a demand center (open to whining from all sides). And true multitasking is actually much more limited in practice than its bandying-about might imply. It turns out that I haven't been multitasking after all. I've been in a state of "continuous partial attention" for the last decade or so, and that's not such a good thing.

In *The Humane Interface*, software philosopher Jef Raskin (1943–2005) argued that the nature of human attention precludes all but the most simple forms of multitasking. Human beings, regardless of age or ability, can actually focus on just one activity at a time. Any additional tasks must be automatic, matters of semiconscious habit rather than ongoing deliberation. I can chop vegetables (semiconscious) and talk to my student (focused and aware), but when the child demands cookies, both flows are broken, and when I fetch the cookies, I am not multitasking. I am simply engaged in a new chore.

Multitasking occupies a certan middle range of experience: good-enough conversation, on-the-go meals, reading for the plot, repetitive crafting, routine sex. Trying to achieve higher order experiences, whether it's philosophy in the bedroom or adultery in the kitchen, while at the same time fiddling with your BlackBerry can lead to frustration or failure.

According to Raskin, it takes humans about ten seconds to shift from one context to another. A person deeply absorbed in an activity such as reading email or fantasizing about rubber handcuffs might take even longer to respond to a new demand. The ten-second rule explains my own annoyance when I'm asked for a cookie as well as my child's rage when I'm slow to respond. In order to support human multitasking, interface designers work to render more tasks automatic (cut and paste, save functions, file retrieval, key commands), decreasing the ten-second lag to near zero.

Driving is a largely automatic process, especially when the driver knows her route. Cell phones, NPR, hot coffee, and screaming children are attention-weeds that flourish in the margins of focus left over by automatic pilot. Yet when the chicken suddenly decides to cross the road, the driver must shift immediately from one context to another. And in that transition accidents can occur. Using a cell phone while driving—whether or not the device is handheld—increases the chance of an accident by 400 percent. Why? Because the mental focus as much as the physical manipulation demanded by the phone competes with the driver's full attention.

Updating a Facebook page while sitting in class or checking email while talking to your mother on the phone is not really multitasking. You are not actually doing two things at once; you are shifting between them. Tech observer Linda Stone coined the phrase "con-

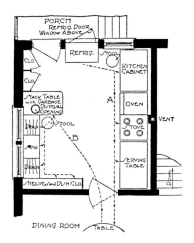

MOTHERS OF THE MODERN KITCHEN
In 1913, Christine Frederick applied Ford's factory model to the modern kitchen. Her workstations and simplified traffic patterns reduced kitchen labor into a linear process, divided into preparing meals and cleaning them up. But is cooking a meal really like building a car? Her predecessor in modern kitchen design, Catharine Beecher, presented a more realistic picture of life in the kitchen: "For a housekeeper's business is not, like that of the other sex, limited to a particular department. It consists of ten thousand little disconnected items, which can never be so systematically arranged that there is no daily jostling somewhere."

tinuous partial attention" to describe the marauding state of constant scanning that characterizes the work and play modes of contemporary life. Although there are moments of the day when this openness to new information keeps you fresh and ready, many productivity experts suggest that the rapturous "flow" of creative work requires a break from over-stimulation. The very companies that brought us ubiquitous computing, including Intel and U.S. Cellular, have instituted Zero Email Fridays. Meanwhile, high-tech productivity-obsessed "life hackers" are increasingly declaring email bankruptcy: deleting their entire inboxes and starting over.

In his classic study of creativity, Mihaly Czikszentmihalyi found that creativity thrives in two kinds of spaces: beautiful, special spots removed from the ordinary, such as a seaside perch or a forest walk, and comfortable, familiar work spaces. The beautiful retreat is often where big ideas take flight, while the routine space is where those ideas get worked out over time into usable results (novels, theories, scientific discoveries).

Does flow mean working in absolute quiet? Not necessarily. (See "Getting Out of the House.") But for most of us, it does mean courting absorption by turning off the demands. Meanwhile, I'll hold on to a few forms of simple multitasking. My favorite: washing my bras in the bathtub. While I'm taking a bath. Yup, I'm right in there with my dirty underwear. But I'm a busy woman, and it gets the job done. **JL**

YOU'RE SOAKING IN IT

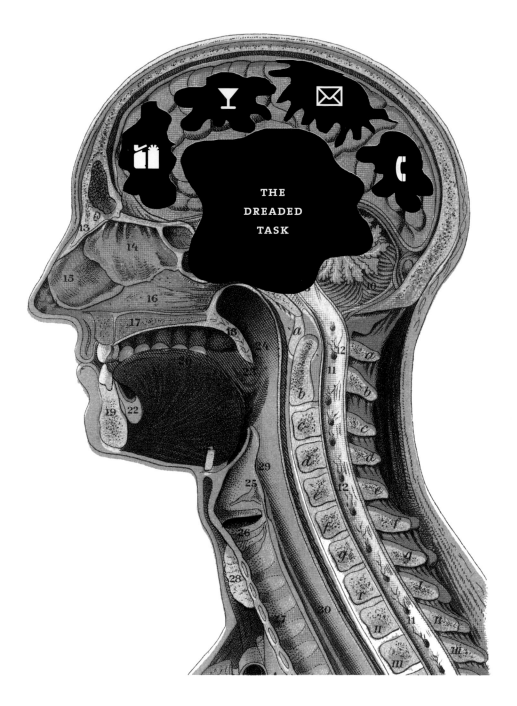

THE DREADED TASK *Like a mysterious astrophysical phenomenon, the object of procrastination exudes a powerful repelling force while threatening to swallow up your entire universe. Irresistible distractions feed on its implosive energy.*

THE ART OF PROCRASTINATION

Procrastination is a mental burden, a leaden ball tethered to an elastic chain. We often dedicate more energy to dreading a project than to actually doing it. Procrastination is a curse, but it is also a craft, a subtle form of creativity. Like any discipline (pole vaulting, rock climbing, or playing solitaire at work), procrastination involves diligence and skill as well as danger and risk.

Although this essay falls right near the middle of this book, it was one of the very last pieces to be produced. For two full years, I avoided sitting down to write about the delicious and distressing art of delay. While avoiding the task, however, I was actually working on it—indirectly. The subject was, I like to say, marinating. Although the outcomes of some tasks will reap no benefit from drawn-out waiting periods (sending a thank-you note or getting a mammogram), others, like writing an essay, can be nourished by a rich layer of mental dust. The conscious act of avoiding a task keeps it vital in your mind, where it can swim about freely, unhindered by tangible action. This fruitful period is a stay of execution, the project's last chance to live before falling under the ruthless knife of implementation.

The more distant the deadline, the longer you can procrastinate, but beware: as with a tart marinade, if you let the meat soak too long in the caustic juices of delay, the whole project could turn to mush. One of the great delusions of the procrastinator is the phrase "If only I had more time." Given more time, most people will put off getting serious about their project that much longer. Often, the most creative work happens near the end, just as time is running out.

Procrastination's dark sister is the deadline. Although some projects will succumb to inertia even under the threat of death, many will meet the mark seconds before the ax falls, frantic but complete. If people did not procrastinate, deadlines would not exist. The ying of delay requires the yang of lethal injection. The deadline holds addictive allure for countless creative people, who thrill at testing its limits, its pliability, and its truth. Could a six-month research study actually be completed in two days? Is your client's deadline a legitimate cut-off point or a mirage of her own making? What will happen if you're late? Will you be humiliated at a staff meeting, get reassigned to a cubicle in southeast Siberia, or receive a new, more realistic deadline? I have often prided myself on completing an urgent task only to wait days, weeks, even months, for a response.

Nearly any self-help book about getting your disordered act together includes a section on to-do lists. (In fact, some such guides are organized as lists, such as Gina Trapani's *Life Hacker: 88 Tech Tricks to Turbocharge Your Life*.) A list is a graphic tool that helps you visualize your priorities. Writing stuff down also helps prevent unfinished tasks from gnawing away at the edges of your mind. Externalizing information keeps it alive while keeping it at bay. The list can acquire a life of its own. I sometimes note a task that is already finished, simply for the reward of obliterating it with my fat black Sharpie.

A list is a database about your life. Such lists have become increasingly public, as groupware programs like Basecamp and Google Docs allow collaborative teams to track their to-do lists online—and view each other's progress. Such tools make people's ability to act (or failure to do so) transparent and visible.

Culturally, public lists function as a measure of accomplishment, a representation of personal taste and knowledge. Lists have flourished as a freestanding literary genre, as seen in John Hodgman's farcical *The Areas of My Expertise*. Amazon's Listmania tool lets users curate lists of books and other goods (and advertise Amazon products). Goodreads is a social website for sharing lists of what users are reading or hope to read. The productivity blog 43Folders suggests warding off distractions by posting a Not-to-Do List over your desk ("Do not search for gray hairs" or "Do not post to your blog").

Where do you keep your lists? And what about all the other notes, reminders, and occasional bolts of joy or genius that strike without warning throughout the day ("get butter," "call dentist," "pet a kitten," "invent wind-powered SUV")? People capture data with everything from BlackBerries to index cards to purpose-made stationery systems. Some of us put all our notes, no matter what the subject, in one place; this mental dumping ground can be anything from a giant searchable Word document to a hand-bound sketchbook. Others prefer to keep a different capture vehicle for each project—a separate slender Moleskine, for example, for "obsessions," "obligations," and "conquests."

The following techniques for taming the clock and stoking creativity reflect a designer and writer's perspective; they are useful for tackling dreaded tasks and duty-soaked schedules of any kind. **EL**

Taming the Clock

BURST CLEANING Working quickly in tiny slivers of time is a housekeeping technique that can be applied to creative work as well. In the ten-minute lull before your mother-in-law arrives for the weekend, you could wipe down your kitchen countertops, organize your junk mail, rid your medicine chests of commonly abused prescription drugs, and compose a haiku about dragonflies and melting snow.

CHUNKING Turn one big job into many small ones. If you have a grossly disordered closet, try starting with just a single category, such as "shoes," "skeletons," "stuff on the floor," or "stuff that shouldn't be in the closet anyway." (Procrastinate on the rest until you're ready to tackle the next chunk.) Similarly, a vast, vague task such as "achieve job satisfaction" becomes manageable when mercilessly hacked into little pieces, such as "send résumé to Bob," "stop sitting next to Fred," and "blow whistle on Jane."

TEA TIME Bach, Balzac, Kant, and Rousseau all did their best work on caffeine. Why can't you? But even better than the new beginning delivered by a good cup are the things you can accomplish while the water is boiling: schedule a root canal, empty the dishwasher, or plot your escape from a loveless marriage.

MENTAL PENCIL SHARPENING When delaying work on a project, try a variety of rituals to prepare the ground for real action later on, such as gathering and digesting research materials, creating charts and diagrams, making relevant and irrelevant phone calls, sending relevant and irrelevant emails, and going shopping. (Nearly any project can be framed to justify a shopping excursion, also known as "research.") When you finally sit down to do the job, the work will have already begun.

EXFOLIATE Moisturizers with retinol (the animal form of vitamin A) force your skin to turn cells over more quickly, revealing softer, firmer cells beneath. You can also exfoliate your closet (out with the old, in with the new), or your cabinets (discard those five-year-old bottles of whole cloves), and your writing (replace tawdry or timid words with sparkly new ones).

DO SOMETHING ELSE Go for a drive, or take a hike, or take a shower; maybe you'll have better luck when you come back to the task later. Furthermore, the act of not doing one thing gives you time to do something else. No matter what project I am working on at any given moment (writing an essay or plotting a pyramid scheme), a corner of my brain is always worrying about something else that I should be doing instead (paying the bills or creating a scale replica of the Parthenon out of cookie dough.)

DON'T DO LUNCH Meetings are powerful time magnets that quickly mushroom into opportunities for procrastination. Lunch makes this problem worse. The so-called working lunch is generously padded with small talk and menu chatter. Keep your meetings short and focused. People tend to schedule meetings in one-hour time blocks, yet many useful discussions can take place in fifteen minutes or less. Participants are less likely to be late for a shorter meeting set for a specific time, such as 3:45.

LOCK YOURSELF IN A ROOM Chuck Berry wrote many of his greatest songs, including "No Place to Go," during a two-year stint in prison.

LIGHTEN UP If you're blocked on a project, remind yourself that "It's just graphic design," "It's only a wedding," or "I didn't really want to go to med school that much anyway."

GET SERIOUS If the blow-it-off approach doesn't work for you, try a rain dance, pow-wow, or recommitment ceremony (to your editor, client, or your future).

TO SHOE OR NOT TO SHOE? *It's a tough call.*

SHOE WARS

My friend Michelle was driving one day with her Pakistani-born husband through a generic suburban development in Florida, looking for the home of another South Asian family. They had a basic idea of where their friends lived but no solid address—and all of the houses looked alike. Suddenly, they saw a pile of shoes heaped around an entryway. "That's it!" they exclaimed, knowing they had arrived.

The custom of slipping off one's shoes before going indoors is commonplace in many parts of the world. In the United States, the practice is becoming more widespread, taking hold among a rising generation attracted to this practical ritual, which not only promotes cleanliness and protects property but also marks a symbolic divide between the hustle of public life and the peaceful remove of the home.

Taking off your shoes is, it would seem, a no-brainer. Grit, grime, and doggy dung carried in from outside damage floors and carpets while spreading potential pestilence. The scuffs and scratches left by street shoes can be difficult, even impossible, to erase. Yet shoe removal is often a site of intense conflict, dividing friends and family along generational and cultural lines. Michelle's own sister refuses to do it, saying "We didn't grow up like that."

Some visitors find it uncomfortable—even unthinkable—to expose one's stocking (possibly stinking) feet outside one's own bedroom. Diabetes and other medical conditions can make it dangerous to walk around barefoot. To the well-heeled set, arriving decked out at a holiday party and being asked to exchange one's fancy footwear for a pair of house slippers feels like a violation of the self. Bewildered and unprepared, a guest can feel embarrassed that she didn't know the rule and annoyed at the pressure to comply. A visitor thrown off balance by shoe confusion may take all evening to regain her footing.

On the other side of the welcome mat, avidly shoeless hosts take offense at people who are unaware of the custom or neglect to observe it. A shoeless house provides clues of its status; guests traveling this newly uncertain terrain are advised to take note of them. A basket of shoes near the front door is an obvious indicator; so is a sign that reads, "Kindly remove your shoes" or, more crudely, "Please keep your dirty shoes off our clean floors." Many newcomers have learned to ask, "Should I take off my shoes?" A merciful host will provide guests with slippers, socks, and a comfortable bench; some will even offer forgiveness to visitors who fail to comply.

New social manners take time to catch on, and it's not clear yet whether this one will ever become a norm in the United States. The last huge sea change in domestic taboos was smoking. Time was when it was actually polite to inquire, "Do you mind if I smoke?" Today, most of us wouldn't dare to ask. Ashtrays have disappeared from the lexicon of respectable household objects. When I was a child, we made them in art class as Mother's Day gifts. Today, my kids barely know what an ashtray looks like. Yet this shift, which has caused far more generational strife than the shoe wars, took decades to solidify.

ASHTRAY OR CANDY DISH? *As an experiment, I recently set out some candy in a vintage ashtray to see what would happen. The transgression went undetected; the kids gobbled up the candy, no questions asked.*

I once held a party for a group of designers from the Netherlands, who smoked like coal-burning factories for three hours in my narrow, poorly ventilated New York City apartment. When I commented on the density of the smoke to one of my guests, he retorted, "You Americans are so worried about smoking and pollution, and yet you drive huge cars to work while we all ride bikes." (Actually, most New Yorkers walk or take the subway, but he was right about Americans overall. We choose our prohibitions carefully.)

What do welcome mats really say? Although inscribed with the word "welcome," their real message is "please wipe your feet." Even without reading the text, most people have learned to give their shoes an extra rub against the bristled surface of an entry mat before coming inside. This functional design object provides a tactful and tactile transition between outdoors and indoors.

How bad would it be if your mother-in-law, your nosy neighbor, or the lady from Child Protection Services refused to remove her Jimmy Choos after invading your home? In my house, guests are a rare enough occasion that I don't mind if some of them slip off their shoes and some of them don't. We have what I call a voluntary shoe policy. Those of us who live here usually have our shoes off. (Our sock-covered feet appear to be effective tools for attracting grime off the floors.) Our guests are welcome to do as they please. **E L**

Bad Manners

Over the past century, rules of civility have become markedly more relaxed in areas such as hats, gloves, and premarital sex, while standards have grown far stricter in some other domains. Below are some snippets from *Manners for Millions*, published in 1932.

CHAPTER 23
SMOKING

IN A home where you do not see any evidence of smoking, it is in good taste to inquire if smoking is objectionable.

Try to smoke in as clean a way as possible. Dropping ashes all over the davenport, the tablecloth, the floor, or any other place is objectionable to the neat housekeeper.

Try not to allow the smoke to blow directly into another's face. (This cannot always be avoided.)

CHAPTER 22
CHEWING GUM

Never give chewing gum to anyone—even to a child—if you have chewed it.

Never take gum from another person's mouth.

WORKING FATHER MAGAZINE

DOES YOUR BOSS KNOW
YOU HAVE KIDS?

PARENTING STYLES:
WHY YOURS IS BETTER

BABY-PROOF YOUR
BLACKBERRY

WANT TO BREAST FEED?
WELL, YOU CAN'T

SOUP TO NUTS:
PLANNING A MEN'S-ONLY
BABY SHOWER

GET YOUR
COLLEGE
BODY BACK:
DRINK MORE
BEER

SPECIAL FEATURE: HOW TO PICK UP YOUR SOCKS

THE DADDY TRACK *While middle-class women have perceived choices about motherhood and work, our society simply assumes that dads have jobs. This concept for a consumer magazine comes from designer dad Abbott Miller.*

THE MYTH OF THE WORKING MOTHER

"How do you do it all?" I often get this question, and my answer is this: no one does it all. "Doing it all" is code for having a career and having kids, and it's one of the great myths of our era. The myth is that you can pursue these two incompatible activities without screwing up either one. The myth is that having children will invigorate your work, and that working will make you a more interesting and fulfilled person, and thus a better parent.

A few years ago, I spoke on a panel of female designers. The panel sought to "offer unique insights on juggling career and family, dealing with stress, and how all the chaos offers training and inspiration for becoming a better designer, a better businessperson, and a better mother." That program blurb neatly summed up the myth, suggesting that the frazzled life of the working mom provides the ultimate training ground for getting better at everything. A question from the audience came from Boston-based designer Fritz Klaetke, who asked why there weren't any men on the panel. After all, having kids takes a toll on their careers, too.

There is a much-reported trend among young, educated, upper-middle class women to opt-out of the workforce. This new generation places more value on devoting time to their kids and less value on professional success. Journalist Judith Warner credits this shift to the realization that society has failed to provide the support systems needed to make "doing it all" truly feasible (including flexible workplaces and affordable childcare). The new "total-reality motherhood"—the belief that small children require constant stimulation and feedback from their parents—has further compelled moms to stay at thome.

A strange conversational dance occurs when two women meet and begin finding out who's a SAHM (stay-at-home mom) and who's a WOHM (work-outside-the-home mom). It's awkward to ask directly, so you look for clues. A mom who wears tennis whites when she drops off the kids at school might not have a job, but you never know; she could be a lawyer with a home office or a brain surgeon who works the night shift. I guess I'm a SAWM: a stay-at-work mom who took the shortest possible maternity leave after each birth.

There's a "mommy war" going on, and members of each side may feel more comfortable with others who have made choices like theirs. Furthermore, we are often eager to validate our own decisions as the best ones for our children. The SAHMs occupy the moral high ground in this matter—they're the ones who have made the big sacrifice, spending crucial years of their lives almost exclusively with their kids, refusing to hand over their babies and toddlers to nannies, au pairs, and day care facilities for eight or ten hours a day.

It seems obvious to me that mothers and fathers are the best "care givers" for small children, and research more or less bears this out. Working moms try to argue that their own kids are getting the better deal: earlier socialization, more independence, an immune system toughened by exposure to pathogens, and, above all, the opportunity to draw inspiration from a busy mother whose personal identity derives not just from her children, but also from a career. But young children are deeply self-involved. Until my kids reached elementary school age, they rarely took interest in either parent, beyond our readiness to entertain, protect, soothe, feed, and transport them. Little kids want to be with their parents because we make them feel safe, whole, and happy, not because they admire our professional achievements.

Despite these truths, I nonetheless decided to continue working while my children were small. They are now in their early teens. What choices will they make? Will they have children? Will they have jobs? (Will jobs exist when they grow up?) Would they have become happier adults if I hadn't worked? I'll never know, any more than I will know what kind of professional success I would have found if I hadn't slowed down to have children.

One day when he was in second grade, my son Jay announced, "Most of my friends' moms don't work." Dismay lurched in my gut. "What do you make of that?" I asked. "I dunno," he said, shrugging.

When asked the same question a few years later, he said he liked my job because I teach him "cool design stuff," like how to use Flash and make websites. My daughter, Ruby, felt similarly. "Mommy, you're cool," she remarked one morning. "Wow," I said. "Why do you think I'm cool?" (Surely it wasn't my Lands' End circle skirt.) "Because you're a designer, and we get to design things together." So my children have found some value in my professional skills. We even published a book together (*D.I.Y. Kids*). They are each finding their own place in the world of art and media. Maybe they'll use their doodles, icons, and avatars to design a better family. **EL**

GET BY WITH A LITTLE HELP FROM YOUR FRIENDS Busy parents often exchange child care and other services with friends and neighbors. Political scientists call these informal networks "social capital," in which people build up credit with each other by returning favors. Larger families, immigrants, and single-parent households are more likely to develop these reciprocal ties than insulated nuclear ones. Remember the old lady who lived in the shoe? (Just how old was she, and how dirty was that shoe?) She would have been better off with a few neighbors around.

How to Spend Less Time with Your Kids

A disturbing trend is evident everywhere: in middle-class households, parents are spending more and more time with their children! In earlier generations, entry into elementary school meant less rather than more parent-child contact. Stay-at-home moms were suddenly free to enjoy martinis, go back to school, or buy a vibrator. Meanwhile, working mothers could devote more hours to the job (or buy a vibrator). Children were known to walk or bike to school and to spend a few hours at home alone in the afternoons. The bottom line: school meant more freedom, for both children and adults. This equation is now at risk, due to an insidious set of trends:

HOMEWORK HELL Despite a lack of statistical correlation between homework and school success, ambitious parents continue to agitate for more assignments. Yet the arrival of homework packets at the beginning of each school week transforms many households into battle zones. Children "win" these battles by holding out as long as possible in the completion of simple assignments that even their dog could eat.

SPORTS PURGATORY Soccer, softball, and swim teams keep kids, and parents, busy. A parent or her representative must drive the child to practices and games and then feign both interest and knowledge during said event. She is also forced to chat with other parents, some of whom may actually know the difference between an Oriole and an Angel. Too much exposure to organized sports can cause bloating, hot flashes, and bad hair days in mothers, while fathers have reported sudden delusions of candor.

KARATE KIDS Despite the physical safety of many suburban settings, exotic self-defense classes (karate, jujutsu, and teriyaki bowl) are on the rise, along with Mom's taxi service. Maybe she could learn some self-defense herself!

TAKE ACTION. These trends are disturbing, but, as with global warming, you can help solve the problem. Do your share to help keep childhood from becoming a chronic condition.

HAVE YOU TRIED TELEVISION? The truth is, parents like it and so do kids. Be sure to have at least two sets so that adults are not needlessly subjected to "family programming." Parceling out TV and Internet privileges in relation to specific responsibilities could solve your homework problems. Consider a modest TV set in the master bedroom; pornography has saved more marriages than it has destroyed.

THAT'S WHY WE LIVE ON A CUL-DE-SAC Wean children from organized sports (or prevent addiction in the first place) by encouraging them to play ball and ride skateboards right at home. If your setting does not support unsupervised outdoor play, try some of the new electronic games that require physical activity. And don't forget: there's always jumping on the bed.

PLAY DATES Just hanging out with other kids may sound old-fashioned when your child could be learning a foreign language or training for the Olympics. Play dates are free, safe, and convenient. Learn the arts of reciprocity and hospitality without special classes or manuals! Daytime play dates among younger kids develop into evening and sleepover arrangements for older ones. And that means more adult time, without the cost of a baby sitter.

THE DINNER HOUR The "hour" part is for the adults (with wine, please), but the first ten minutes can be safely shared with the kids. If you're not on taxi duty all afternoon, there's more time to make a real meal. The kids can set the table, then share their days with the grown-ups. It's not pretty, but they do eat quickly. Once they've cleared their plates, let them watch TV. In another room.

HELICOPTER PARENT *Kids and adults alike are under constant surveillance.*

HOMELAND SECURITY

Alert: code pink and blue. A war is being waged to keep America's children safe. To protect our smallest civilians, manufacturers have prepared an arsenal of specialized devices, including nanny cams, safety gates, and toilet seat locks. Outside, sexual predators are ready to snatch your children off playgrounds and public restrooms. Rest assured: the justice system is developing sophisticated means, including GPS navigation and retinal scans, to help you keep track of sex offenders. (Who's next? The parents who don't check the lists?) Don't forget that there's safety in numbers: organized sports are safer than informal play on scooters and bikes. Easier just to keep your kids inside? Television is a source of dangerous stimuli, and the Internet is simply another portal for pederasty. The most important weapon, however, against all these dangers is the constant state of alert delivered by the onslaught of the evening news.

An astonishing range of child-safety devices hits the market each year—most are destined to hit the landfills a heartbeat later. High-tech features promise to regulate the low-tech processes of eating, sleeping, and pooping. Why settle for a hand-me-down baby monitor when you can get a voice-activated crib light that plays soothing womb sounds? How about an indoor safety gate with an alarm that goes on when you forget to shut it, or a digital wrist watch that sets off a mini sound-and-light show to remind your toddler to use the toilet? (Yes, this stuff is real.) Devices such as a sleek electric infant scale that keeps track of baby's weight gain are marketed to the ever-more-watchful mom in a culture of constant surveillance from both inside and outside the home. The bottom line: Never leave your child unattended. Ever.

When I was in college, I never imagined having more than two children. Half a decade spent fighting infertility, however, led to a bonanza of babies. When our first daughter was born, we gamely sampled the many products and services that circle each phase of infant development like so many child-proofed sharks. Nursing chairs, nursing pillows, and breast pumps. Flash cards for newborns. Tiny gyms for tummy time. Mommy and Me musical enrichments for a baby who couldn't sing (and a mommy with no ear).

Everything changed when our triplets were born three years later. Not only did bottles and formula pollute the pristine lactational landscape, but those bottles were—egads—propped! We learned to unplug the nursery monitor and let the babies cry it out as a team.

During a recent sex ed event at my fifth-grader's school, a brief unit informing kids about the dangers of sexual abuse ballooned into lurid scenarios of kidnapping and predation. Although the facilitator emphasized that 90 percent of abuse issues from adults whom kids already know, the fantasy that fueled the room was one of scheming strangers. The presentation, which never turned to topics such as body image, had been effectively kidnapped. Although child abduction cases have been declining since the early 1990s, the pervasive fear culture prevents many parents from letting their kids walk down the block alone. Meanwhile, childhood obesity is a real and present danger, not a fabricated one.

Audrey van Buskirk, a new mother and freelance writer, reported in *Portland Life* that her new Graco Snugride came with nineteen separate warning labels. Risks include suffocation (the plastic bag), strangulation (by the straps), finger entrapment (base-to-seat), and beverage burns (mom's coffee in baby's cup holder. Duh?). Depending on whom you ask, between 88 and 99 percent of car seats are installed incorrectly. The good news: the major problem is strap tightness. Follow the one-inch rule: the seat shouldn't budge more than an inch in any direction, and tolerate no more than an inch of pinch when you strap baby in her seat. Just how hard is it anyway? The Alliance for Community Traffic Safety offers a 32-hour course to train professionals in car-seat checks. Yet parents are supposed to get it right on their own. Because of liability concerns, it's harder and harder to get someone in the store or maternity ward to check your seat.

There is a growing domestic insurgency among households resistant to excessive child-proofing. Child psychologist Wendy Mogel, confronted by mounting anxiety spikes in the under-twelve set, has urged families to take the minor scrapes of life as opportunities for talk and growth, not fear and trembling. A child who learns how to negotiate corners may be a more resilient adult two decades from now. Kids who grew up behind the safety gates are now having children themselves, and many are saying "No" to the lock-and-key regime of their risk-reduced childhoods. Some adults are training children to navigate table edges and stemware instead of coating their kids' world in brightly colored plastic. Households are reducing gadget turnover by adjusting habits and routines rather than buying new products as children crawl, toddle, and walk around the house.

Will these more relaxed forms of parenting lead to a rise in accidents? Perhaps. But the safety wars may have trained the culture to monitor real risks, like choking, lead, and inadequate seat belts. (Not to mention poverty and global warming.) Meanwhile, maybe we can place the lurid specters of stranger abduction and strangulation by car seat into the background where they belong, along with monsters under the bed, spiders in the bathroom, and a C in second-grade science. My own cul-de-sac kids, ages seven to eleven, are venturing beyond the cozy curve of the asphalt nest and exploring the neighborhood streets on their bikes and scooters. My heart is firmly buckled to my throat, but no safety gate will keep them inside now. **JL**

PADDED CELL Crib bumpers were initially designed to protect babies from sticking their heads through the wide slats of cribs. Tough crib standards in the U.S. and Canada have decreased this risk to almost zero. In the meantime, crib bumpers have been linked to Sudden Infant Death Syndrome (SIDS). The crib bumper remains, however, a beloved element of nursery decor, as expectant parents busily furnish their nests with matching fabrics. A bare bed, however, is safer than a padded cell. The best crib ornament, it turns out, is a fresh baby (ideally a drowsy one), packaged in a snug sleeper suit.

HOLIDAYS
AND
HOSPITALITY

SILENT FRIGHT *We love the down time, the family time, and even the fruitcakes.*
But the ceaseless Christmas music is driving us crazy.

THE PERMANENT HOLIDAY

Ever since its birth in the Middle Ages, Christmas has lasted a season, not a day. Advent is the pre-Christmas fast—essentially a long diet before the revelry to come. Then there are the Twelve Days of Christmas, which fall after, not before, the 25th. Behind these waning favorites are the ghosts of calendars past. For many centuries, for example, January 1 marked the Feast of the Circumcision, honoring the bris or ritual circumcision of Jesus. (This holiday was instituted by the Church to combat the extreme partying of the Roman New Year.)

Thus Christmas has always had elastic borders, but its stretchiness was designed to accommodate the distinctive moments and symbols of the Christmas story itself—as well as the emotional needs of sun-starved peasants living in an economy of scarcity. Now Christmas is all abundance, no lack. Yet our horns of plenty hide carbon footprints that are stopping the Abominable Snowman and his reindeer too, right in their Arctic tracks, and our giant stockings stuffed with disposable goodies are the fruit of global labor practices that no one wants to talk about around the electric tree.

When, exactly, do the "holidays" start? Halloween has always lurked at the far edge of the Christmas season. Since Shocktober advertising starts when the little monsters go back to school, the holiday sales push gets going as early as September and keeps marching on through January (the month of final markdowns and last returns). Just when we thought Christmas was finally over, its fading colors are reflected one last time in the red light district of Valentine's Day. That's one long shopping season.

The merging of Christmas into the generic "holidays" flat lines its vital functions. Holiday shopping is as old as—holidays and shopping. Yet even the most dedicated consumers are beginning to revolt at the prospect of Christmas in July. Anthropologists suggest that the purpose of holidays is to create a momentary break from the tedium of daily life. When holidays become permanent, we end up yearning for a holiday from holidays as such. Please, please, please: let me go back to work!

Just to keep the bells jingling, every few decades there's a War Against Christmas. The Puritans hated the pagan roots of Christmas, so they banned Saint Nick from the Massachusetts Bay Colony. A New England Christmas, it seems, is not so classic after all. In 1959, the John Birch Society accused the "godless UN" of conspiring with department stores to destroy Christmas with excessive consumerism. A few years ago, Christian conservatives took up arms against the liberalism of the phrase "Happy Holidays," advising the faithful to shop only at stores that greeted their guests with a properly Godly "Merry Christmas." Unlike their predecessors, the main theme of these modern boycotters was not *whether* to shop, but *where* to shop.

Maybe the real issue, though, is not "Christmas" versus "Holidays," but "Merry" versus "Happy." The demand to be happy at a time of year when the days are short and moods are blue feels unrealistic and even cruel. But the call to be merry simply enjoins your minimal consent to the scripted cheer of sugar, fat, alcohol, and extra time with your relatives. After all, you can be merry (drunken, obnoxious, sarcastic, even mean) without being the least bit happy.

Meanwhile, the new crafting movement is stealing holidays back from the Grinch of consumerism by populating a strange, vast underworld with evil Easter eggs, sick Santas, and snowballs from Hell. All this handicrafting is also mental labor and social work, addressing the futures of the holidays themselves as part of a larger global scene. When creating Christmas angels from virgin tampons, the craftista must contemplate the icons of Yuletide with a certain icy tenderness in order to balance spunk and spleen, clever repurposing with the just plain gross. For the new crafters, every holiday is a form of Halloween, an assemblage of ghosts from feast days past who are eager to take back the night with glue guns, eyelet presses, and a few red and green Sharpie pens.

I've made a truce with Christmas. Having converted to Judaism some years ago, I send my kids to Jewish day school, where I've learned that Hanukah is simply Christmas by other means. I am perfectly happy to have Christians take back Christmas. I'd just like them to do it properly: remove it from our public places and please take care of its magnificent archive of images and symbols. Together, we can make holidays safe, legal, and rare. Fight holiday sprawl by shopping later and buying less. And combat calendar-fatigue by pulling old holidays out of the closet. Feast of the Circumcision, anyone? **JL**

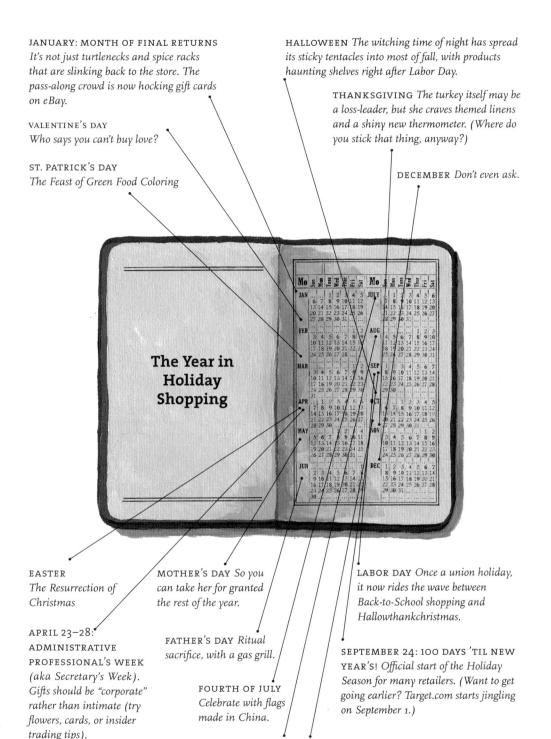

JANUARY: MONTH OF FINAL RETURNS
It's not just turtlenecks and spice racks that are slinking back to the store. The pass-along crowd is now hocking gift cards on eBay.

VALENTINE'S DAY
Who says you can't buy love?

ST. PATRICK'S DAY
The Feast of Green Food Coloring

HALLOWEEN *The witching time of night has spread its sticky tentacles into most of fall, with products haunting shelves right after Labor Day.*

THANKSGIVING *The turkey itself may be a loss-leader, but she craves themed linens and a shiny new thermometer. (Where do you stick that thing, anyway?)*

DECEMBER *Don't even ask.*

The Year in Holiday Shopping

EASTER
The Resurrection of Christmas

APRIL 23–28:
ADMINISTRATIVE PROFESSIONAL'S WEEK
(aka Secretary's Week). Gifts should be "corporate" rather than intimate (try flowers, cards, or insider trading tips).

MOTHER'S DAY *So you can take her for granted the rest of the year.*

FATHER'S DAY *Ritual sacrifice, with a gas grill.*

FOURTH OF JULY
Celebrate with flags made in China.

GEAR UP FOR BACK TO SCHOOL SHOPPING *Lunch boxes absorb the ghosts of grades past and require annual exorcism.*

LABOR DAY *Once a union holiday, it now rides the wave between Back-to-School shopping and Hallowthankchristmas.*

SEPTEMBER 24: 100 DAYS 'TIL NEW YEAR'S! *Official start of the Holiday Season for many retailers. (Want to get going earlier? Target.com starts jingling on September 1.)*

OCTOBER 16: BOSS'S DAY.
Usually honored with a small gift or joke card; you might also try a simple lawsuit.

CHOCOLATE FOUNTAIN IN WOODLAND SETTING

MISGIVINGS

Once upon a time, back in the early 1970s, my mother-in-law received a vacuum cleaner as a birthday gift from her husband. She was not amused. The brand name of this mechanical dust-sucker was Regina, and to convey her scorn she referred to the device ever after as the *Raj-*EYE-*nah* (rhymes with "vagina").

Some domestic appliances do make appropriate gifts: those involved with cooking, for example, can suggest creative self-expression and social togetherness. A family might exclaim with glee at the perfectly pulverized onions churned out by a new food processor, or perhaps they will gather happily in the winter months around a simmering Crock-Pot. It is more difficult, however, to imagine wringing pleasure from a self-cleaning steam iron or a 1400-watt Regina.

When giving a small appliance to a friend or loved one, consider the space it will consume as well as the ratio between its potential usefulness and the burden of maintaining it. A fondue set, for example, might only be employed a few times a year. Is the task of removing it from the deepest, darkest corner of the pantry and putting it back after use sufficiently rewarded by the joy of communing with one's kin around a bubbling vat of molten cheese?

One object that surely fails this test is the chocolate fountain. This spectacular device appears at retailers everywhere during the months before Christmas. Its purpose is to astound party guests with a tiered waterfall of liquid chocolate, into which they dip chunks of strawberry, pineapple, and vintage fruitcake. A brown fountain is an astonishing sight indeed, as is the vision of small children smeared head to toe with sticky, indelible muck. But is all that joy worth the trauma of cleaning up? It turns out that you are not supposed to wash a chocolate fountain directly in your kitchen sink, because the chocolate can harden up and clog your plumbing pipes. (The same is true for melted cheese.) So, the unlucky hostess is advised to disassemble the fountain and wipe down its parts with warm water and paper towels. Better yet, return to sender.

Another object to avoid is the joke gift, a category that includes t-shirts imprinted with embarrassing messages, children's toys presented inexplicably to adults, and bars of soap engraved with the word "bitch." The sole purpose of these clever novelties is to elicit a laugh upon the occasion of their opening. As a rule, joke gifts reflect the wit of the giver at the expense of the receiver. Once the wrapping paper and packaging have been thrown away and that strained burst of laughter has passed away, such gifts get consigned to the valley of tears (aka the landfill).

Some of the best presents are the ones that disappear. Cash certainly falls in this category; a fistful of dollars makes an appropriate gift for graduates and other people who are younger than you. (Not so good for your best friend's third marriage to an investment banker.) Avoid gifts that the recipient will feel obligated to display in her home for three and a half months before quietly burying in her yard.

What most gifts have in common—whether good, bad, or ridiculous—is that they exist as something extra. They offer surplus value, beyond what someone simply needs, in the form of luxury, surprise, or sentimental feeling. The bluntly utilitarian character of a vacuum cleaner makes it an unappealing gift. Likewise, a pack of Kraft American Singles or a roll of toilet paper, no matter how useful, is a poor hostess offering, whereas an exotic candy bar is a pleasing one. Among the best presents I ever received was a set of ninety-six Sharpies in assorted weights and colors. This gift was both useful and luxurious—and it won't last forever. **EL**

COLD CASH MOUNTAIN

BUBBLING CHEESE NATIONAL PARK AND SPA

Dear PTA President,

I appreciate your hard work conscripting three hundred mothers into a sales brigade for the Sally Fluster Giftwrap Company each year to raise money for our kids' school.

I am writing to tell you that I just can't face another round of taking your catalog to the office and around the block, collecting checks in advance and delivering the goods a month later, wrapping gifts all year in the Hanukkah paper that I overbought in November, and winning valuable prizes in exchange for unpaid labor.

I don't know who Sally Fluster is, but I wish she would make her own friends. I lost mine last year when I pressured them to buy paper from my kids instead of theirs.

At our house, we try to recycle gift bags from birthday parties. We also make our own wrapping paper by using spreads from the *LA Times*, and we enjoy adding homemade stickers, colored masking tape, and old crossword puzzles to brown shipping boxes. (Homework works well, too.)

You'll find the money I've saved on wrapping paper this year in the enclosed check. Please note that it's made out directly to the PTA. Sally won't get her usual cut on this one.

Sincerely,

MOTHER RECLAIMING HER DIGNITY

Micro Giving: The New Charity

Hurricane Katrina inspired a flood of giving—but the outpouring led to controversy for the Red Cross, whose decision to reserve some funds for rainy days yet to come frustrated donors. In the wake of the deluge, more people want their money to travel fast to the target of their choice. Here are some current trends in charity. They all share the same desire to give small, act fast, and fly direct.

STRAIGHT DONATIONS Sending a check directly to the charity of your choice cuts out the middle men involved in candy drives and benefit dinners—deleting the so-called premiums that promote tooth decay and landfills. (Your whole donation will be tax-deductible.)

D.I.Y. FUNDRAISING Do you want to turn your jog around the park into a pink ribbon marathon? Reroute your wedding gifts into donations for Darfur? Turn your diet into a hunger fast to raise funds for the homeless? Firstgiving.com and other D.I.Y. charity sites will help you set up a web page for events large and small. Customized charity drives are especially useful for local causes such as raising funds for a family hit by illness.

MICRO LENDING Muhammad Yunus won the 2006 Nobel Peace Prize for his work in micro financing, which involves making small loans directly to impoverished entrepreneurs, from street beggars to shop owners. Web-based organizations allow individuals to make a micro loan to a needy business owner. (Many are women.) Check out grameenfoundation.org and kiva.org.

DIRECT DEMOCRACY It's not about voting; it's about fast and effective fund-raising from a rapidly ramifying digital base. Words count, too. MySpace pages and Facebook Friends visualize social networks and encourage just about anyone to give her two cents.

SMALL FARMING FOR DOLLARS Eating food grown locally supports small farms. CSA (Community Supported Agriculture) is a subscription service that matches area farmers with consumers hungry for fresh produce and a communal connection. When a school or other organization sponsors a subscription drive, it becomes a fund-raiser. Would you rather get a weekly box of organic veggies, or the latest issue of *Golf Digest*? Take a look at localharvest.org/csa/

WORDS FOR RICE Free Rice (freerice.com) is an Internet vocabulary game run by the United Nations. For each word you nail, the UN donates 20 grains of rice to needy populations across the globe. The grains are paid for by advertisers whose banners flash across the bottom of the screen.

MAZZLES: *Two heads, two hands, four feet, six faces*

STRANGE STUFFIES

Mazzles is a homemade stuffed animal. Crudely sewn out of gray felt, he has two simple bulbous heads. Mazzles has no legs, but lucky for him, he has four feet, and each foot has a face. Thanks to the new crafting movement, exotic mutations like Mazzles have infiltrated the toy scene, introducing unprecedented biodiversity into the world of stuffed animals. Felt robots. Siamese rabbits. Monstrous Easter eggs. One-eyed blobs in desperate need of orthodontics.

Such toys have crawled into our houses from neither zoo nor rain forest, but from the world of digital drawing, whose vectored shapes, fierce colors, and permanent states of emergency nurture graphic violence, or just plain graphics, in innocent toys. Yet the viciousness is only fuzz-deep. Although you can encounter some genuinely mean toys out there, even the most befanged creature has incisors made of felt. There is something vegetarian, even *vegetal*, about these tiny pillows of eyeballed fabric. Behind every stuffed lightning bolt key chain lies a baby carrot just waiting to be loved.

Mazzles' heads and feet are actually pseudopods, amorphous projections of felt that protrude gently from his shapeless body. Toys like Mazzles are more akin to the primitive life-forms of the larva, the tumor, and the microbe than to the more advanced evolutionary states marked by the puggle or your local state representative. In the new culture of toys, Bambi doesn't meet Godzilla. Instead, Bambi turns into an ameoba. The new stuffies reveal the truth about plushies: whatever their proclaimed species, at heart, they're always invertebrates.

Mazzles lives online, where his designer, "maz78," has posted him on Craftster.org. Mazzles is not for sale. Rather, both creature and creator are part of a growing online community of amateur toy-makers who share, swap, and sometimes sell their stuffies to each other, and to the occasional *toyeur* like me. Although Mazzles is sweetly primitive, many of these toys are quite sophisticated. On CustomToyLab. com, contributors offer their wares as prototypes for future product lines. There is only one Mazzles, but his digital nest allows monster lovers anywhere to appreciate his fuzzy charm, share his picture with their friends, and even try making one for themselves.

There is a politics to these toys. Each hand-sewn, two-headed rabid squirrel stages a miniature protest against child labor, mass media, meat-eating, global warming, and the terrible indignity of not being able to move out of your parents' house. The affection for malformed creatures gives a new face (or two, or three) to those D.I.Y. artists who might feel a bit misshapen themselves. Making your own monsters may be a way of remaking your self, and crocheting a community in the process.

Can the digital generation save the world one radioactive octopus at a time? Probably not. Sewing your own monster iPod cozy out of felt made in China hardly solves the global labor problem. Moreover, the contemporary mass market sucks up emergent ideas like a giant green slime mold sewn out of polar fleece. I recently bought a one-eyed blob stuffie at an airport Starbucks; critters like Mazzles have mutated into the mainstream.

Although toys can't repair the damage done by grown-ups, it may well be that never before in human history have personal choices (what to buy, what to wear, what to eat, what to make, what to throw away) carried such potential impact. Each mouse click is like the flap of an embroidered butterfly wing. Although these new plushies will cost you more than a teddy bear at Target, consider adopting a monster next time you need a baby gift or a graduation present. You'll earn points for hipness, and you'll be supporting underground designers. Better yet, make one yourself. With your slimy misfit friends. **JL**

POLYPHEMOS IN FLEECE This one-eyed monster was created by Jennifer Bennett Gubicza, a graphic designer turned indie toy maker.

Microbranding

Along with mutant veggie dogs, robotic penguins, and great striped sharks, the crafting movement is spawning a multitude of business models for crafters with their bug-eyes fixed on the long tail market.

THE CRAFTISTA This hipster hocks one-of-a-kind critters on Etsy.com. By reading articles on Etsy on topics such as "The Art of Pricing," "The Theory of Discounting," and "Global Microbrands," the Craftista can pick up a business education while she's designing her bottle cap jewelry line.

THE MOMSTER It all begins with a pile of baby booties and the unconditional boredom of infancy. As her kids get walking shoes, Momster's crafting blossoms into a home-based business, thanks to the digital marketplace and the million tendrils of the mommy blogosphere. Most Momsters are still just earning pin money, though. Meanwhile, a predatory crafting industry enlists mothers in piece work that pays little and can even land them in debt. On the horizon: revenge of the Giant Lactating Squid?

THE SELF-STARTER This savvy seamster has an art school education. She is an artist-entrepreneur who's not afraid to let her toys grow up. She has a serious day job in the design field, and now she's using all the marketing skills she learned in the "real world" to build her own toy business, one felt fang at a time.

THE MAINSTREAMER This cross-over artist has managed to migrate his strange stuffies from their subterranean habitat to soap emporia, paperies, museum shops, and even big box stores. Serious training as a designer or illustrator and some connections with the art toy world helped his deviant toys make the evolutionary leap into normalcy.

THE IDENTITY ARTIST This indie toy maker is really a graphic designer in fake fur. She may sell a few toys, but she also markets her design services to small businesses. Her stylized toys sit alongside cards, stationery, and messenger bags (complete with messages). For the Identity Artist, a successful stuffie is simply a brand gone all soft and three-dimensional.

THE GRAPHIC NOVELIST This creator learned his craft writing comic books, and his 3-D critterati flaunt a graphic flattitude. Bright colors, simple frontal designs, and a diminuitive "mascot" size reveal these creatures' evolutionary path from print into fabric.

THE ORGANIC INTELLECTUAL This provocateur is knitting a brand-new politics out of renewable fibers, recycled silk, and felted sweaters. A passionate blogger, she uses the Internet to build discourses, not sell stuff. Part of the "buy handmade" movement, she's also not afraid to use the word "theory." If the Craftista is an avid congregant in the Church of Craft, the Organic Intellectual is one of its high priests and publicists. Together, they're helping to make craft into the latest religion in America's historic patchwork of Presbyterian, Unitarian, and vegetarian experiments with civil society.

How to Make Your Own Strange Stuffies

HALF-MOON MONSTERS

Monsters can be sweet, cuddly, and curious. Kids ages seven and up as well as multi-thumbed adults can easily design and sew these misfit creatures, each made from a circle of fabric folded in half. See how many different life-forms you can make from one basic pierogi shape. Treat your half moon as a face or a fishy body. Try turning it upside down for a view from the bottom. Before you sew the sides together, add a few eyes and a mouth. To amp up the wow! factor, attach tentacles, fins, or a tail.

> SUPPLIES
> *fleece or felt*
> *scissors, needle, thread*
> *buttons or puff balls for eyes*
> *yarn, pipe cleaners, and other random decorations*
> *stuffing*

1. Trace a circle on a piece of felt or fleece.

2. Cut out the circle and fold it in half.

3. Add eyes and other features. You can sew or stick them on with fabric glue or hot glue. Features can also be embroidered using thread, yarn, or embroidery floss.

4. Sew around the curved edge. Use a straight stitch (in and out) or a blanket stitch (loop around the edge). Sew any extra appendages between the two layers as you go.

> Add-ons include:
> FLOPPY EARS (soft fleece)
> HORNS (felt)
> ANTENNAE (pipe cleaners)
> TAIL (strip of fabric or length of ribbon or yarn)
> FINS (triangles of felt or fleece)
> KITTY EARS (cut out a triangle and fold the sides in)
> TEDDY EARS (pinch the ends of half circle and stitch)
> TENTACLES (try knobby multi-colored yarn)

5. Before you get to the end, add stuffing, and then sew shut.

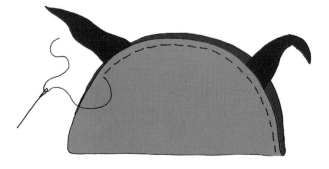

Half-Moon Monsters designed by Izzy, age seven, and Hannah, age eleven.

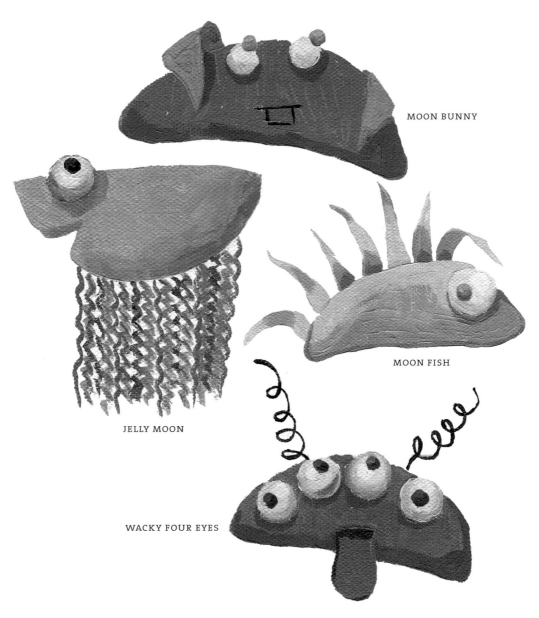

MOON BUNNY

MOON FISH

JELLY MOON

WACKY FOUR EYES

PIN-CUSHION MONSTERS
Try this variation as well. Make a tiny pillow with a scrap of fabric. Add eyes, tails, limbs and other features to create strange and surprising beings with simple bodies. Pin-cushion monsters designed by Ruby, age nine.

SEX

MOTHERHOOD

THE SEX LIFE OF FLOWERS

Flowers are the sexual organs of plants. To cut a blossom from a bush is to deflower it. A bouquet proffers a veritable orgy of genitals, making flowers a classic courtship gift. Hostesses like bouquets, too, which are ready to be thrown out just when one's getting tired of them.

Potted plants and artificial blooms offer more permanent pleasures. Yet potted plants are burdened by too much reality, while fake flowers suffer from too little. An African violet soon shrinks if left unwatered, while its silk facsimile requires dusting. Both saddle their recipient with responsibilities that far outweigh the importance of the occasions that elicit flowers in the first place: a major dinner, a minor birthday, a post-coital forget-me-not.

The melancholy of flowers lies in their mortality. We expect the blooms in a bouquet to fade; transience is part of their charm. A potted plant, however, perishes because *you* have killed it. As for artificial flowers, they positively refuse to die. Promising eternal youth, nothing ages a room, or its hostess, sooner than an urn of silk peonies. Claiming squatters' rights on a side board or coffee table, fake flowers soon collect yesterday's mail-order catalogs and tomorrow's disappointments around their sullen basketry. Tossing a browning bouquet into the trash is a refreshing routine, like flossing your teeth. Throwing out a dusty clump of silk blooms, on the other hand, requires both will and courage, like scheduling a root canal.

The potted plant, its roots stolidly sucking up water from its matronly basin, is positively impervious to erotic imaginings. A foil-swathed chrysanthemum suits a Mother's Day table, but it deals death to the tender shoots of desire sought on Valentine's Day; its appearance as a spousal birthday gift is the sure sign that a marriage has entered its late, chaste stages.

No one even pretends that fake flowers carry an erotic scent. Men rarely buy them, since their florid stems are native to the shelves and buckets of craft stores. Artificial ficus trees thrive on the equally artificial light of middle-management office suites, where their charm is as short as their tenancy is long. **JL**

The Language of Flowers

For centuries, flowers carried symbolic
meanings whose waning scent
can still be detected today.

DAISY

NARCISSUS

ALSTROMERIA

CARNATION

CALLA LILY

ROSE

	Then	Now
CARNATION	Short for "Incarnation," the red ones signified Christ's Passion. These gentle flowers never recovered from the heavy symbolism, but they managed to survive by attaching themselves to Mother's Day (America), Parents' Day (Korea), and final exams (Great Britain).	"I just couldn't stop thinking about you while I was at the grocery store."
ROSE	Love and passion.	"I knew you'd be angry if I didn't buy you roses."
ALSTROMERIA	Devotion and friendship.	"Sorry, but you don't rate roses."
DAISY	Innocence, but also dissembling (just to keep those Renaissance courtiers on their toes).	"You really don't rate roses!"
NARCISSUS	The Greeks fancied that a young man who fell in love with his own reflection turned into this heavy-headed shore-dweller.	"I bought these for myself, because I am so fabulous."
CALLA LILY	Favored in Diego Rivera murals and upscale wedding bouquets, Katherine Hepburn said of them, "Such a strange flower—suitable to any occasion."	"I don't really like flowers, so I got you these weird things instead."

GAWKY

VOLUPTUOUS

The Basic Bouquet

Avoid depositing a store-bought bouquet directly into a vase, where the tight, upright chunk of flowers resembles a guy on a blind date. Instead, cut all the ends to increase water draw, and then place each bloom into the vase separately. The result will be fuller and more relaxed, like a good friend after a fine meal.

While you're at it, consider cutting the stems quite short, and then arrange them in a low, wide-mouthed vase. Store bouquets come tall so that they can catch your attention in the check-out line, but compact arrangements last longer and won't block the view on a dinner table.

GIFT HINT: *Giving your hostess flowers already arranged in a vase will save her needless flurry when she is finishing dinner and greeting guests. Better yet, bring wine or chocolate.*

DON'T SAY IT WITH FLOWERS

TABLE ARRANGEMENTS *can be made out of anything: fruits and gourds; stones and seashells; lemons and light bulbs.*

NOTE: *The day's mail and the morning paper don't count as table arrangements.*

MEAL PLAN. *Flowers are often brought to sick rooms, where they are meant to cheer people up, yet their funereal associations can be a downer, and they require maintenance and disposal. If a household you know is dealing with illness, consider bringing a meal (home-cooked or carry-out) to the house instead.*

OPEN-CASKET BUFFET *The funeral bak'd meats did coldly furnish forth the wedding table.*

SERVING
SUGGESTIONS

"Thrift, thrift, Horatio! The funeral bak'd meats did coldly furnish forth the wedding table." Hamlet lobs these lines at a school chum who has come to Denmark for the funeral of Hamlet's father. Alas, the friend has arrived just as Hamlet's mother is marrying his father's brother (and murderer). The lines are spiked with enough irony to make even the most upbeat hostess pause her ice crusher.

Sure, no one's going to set a wedding table with food from the funeral parlor. Still, doesn't every buffet carry just a whiff of death warmed over? Prepared in a remote location, resurrected from the deep freeze, or kept on life support for hours in chafing dishes, major party foods suffer a time lag between preparation and presentation; their time, as Hamlet would say, is "out of joint." Yet these trays and steam tables, with their forced smiles and flagging garnishes, are summoned against all odds to sustain the powerful present tense of ritual and celebration. The wedding ceremony culminates in the contractual miracle of "I do." A sense of betrayal often follows when the food appears at last in its shiny coffins of elevated steel.

Restrained and tasteful buffet arrangements can help keep the phantoms at bay (ghosts are notoriously attracted to table skirts and Bunsen burners). But a severely minimalist setting can haunt the table with reverse nostalgia, inviting specters of a more gracious time, when seraphs and serifs alike dwelled in the ruffles and signage of the bounteous board. Yes, banish the frou frou—but remember that a few folds of fabric, a length of ivy, or a bit of basketry can revive a table deadened by stacks of square plates and demanding food.

The word "buffet" initially referred to a sideboard, designed not to feed the masses, but rather to show off gold and silver vessels, symbols of solvency in the *ancien regime*. With the rise of the bourgeoisie in the nineteenth century, the term gradually attached itself to the mode of self-service itself, which began as a feature of the breakfast room and only later became an acceptable form for evening dining. Today, a home buffet cuts down labor, encourages circulation, and saves valuable real estate in the eating area. Buffets no longer require a dedicated sideboard; a folding table, dining room table, kitchen counter, or other flat surface can get the job done, as long as there is plenty of room for guests to move. The best buffet is a traffic island, not a dead-end street. Buffets, by nature eclectic, can happily house store-bought goods with home-cooked dishes—Hamlet's "funeral baked meats" next to maiden-voyage casseroles. Vast trays can be punctuated by tiny dishes of brightly colored condiments or salads. Desserts and beverages work best at their own stations.

Plating—the assemblage of plates in the kitchen before serving—is often suited to smaller gatherings in search of formality. While a successful buffet communicates abundance and invite guests to design their own meals, plating casts the chef as the author and curator of a more conscious eating experience. (Take orders in advance to ward against allergy episodes or food fear.) You don't need to carve swans out of radishes in order to compose an attractive plate. It's enough to consider a pleasing ratio of tastes, colors, and textures. Keep portions modest: like a well-designed page, an appealing plate often includes some white space. Many guests would prefer to ask for seconds of that delicious cauliflower surprise than be asked to preside over a burial mound of chow.

"Family-style" service brings the buffet right to the table, in large plates and dishes outfitted for direct access. Whereas plating food implies a degree of decorum, distance, and courtship—among ingredients, dishes, and guests—family-style dining celebrates the marriage, amalgamation, and remixing of foods and people. To some over-scheduled households, "family" and "style" may seem like mutually exclusive ideas. Why bother putting food in tureens and serving dishes when the little barbarians treat their plates as troughs? If every grand buffet, like Hamlet's, risks being haunted by ghosts of weddings past and divorces future, mid-week leftovers mirror mid-life marriages that have "let themselves go." At weeknight feedings, exhausted cooks are known to slap down food directly from cook pots, take-out containers, or yesterday's microwaved Tupperware in order to save time and just get the whole dinner thing over with.

"Thrift, thrift, Horatio"—but at what cost? Order and beauty can find a place at the table along with motorized elbows, outside voices, and homework goblins. There's no need to go the extra mile—a mere inch of extra thought can sweeten the mood and salt the appetite. Simply transferring a carry-out or carry-forward dinner to a favorite serving dish can lay the spirits of the dead to rest while brightening the table with a precious sense of hope. Even on Wednesdays. **JL**

CLASSIC DRAPE This old catering trick creates a variety of levels on the table in order to generate visual drama as well as varied access to the food. First, dress the table with a base cloth. Next, place one or more low, sturdy boxes on top of the main table linen. Swathe the boxes with artfully draped pieces of complementary textiles to build tiny stages for food and flowers.

The Art of the Buffet

FALLING WATER Cut the frills, and use bricks, blocks, planks, slabs of granite, and other materials to create modernist elevations for minimalist meals.

Design Your Plate

Arranging food on individual plates in the kitchen is a restaurant technique suitable for home dinner parties. Plating creates drama and formality as well as portion control. Line, color, pattern, and height can add life to a plate immobilized by meat. Boneless chicken breast needs all the help it can get.

TIME FOR CHICKEN The square meal is really round: served on a basic circle, the starch stands at ten o'clock, the meat at two o'clock, and the vegetables anchor the plate at six o'clock.

TOWER OF CHICKEN Upscale restaurants charge more for food stacked high on the plate. You can build height into your own entree by placing the main element on a bed of greens or a mound of mush.

CHICKEN NAPOLEON A traditional "Napoleon" is a layered pastry. Today, the term is applied to any artful stack of food elements.

FLAG OF CHICKEN Even ordinary food feels more modern when laid out in stripes. Unify the design with a ribbon of sauce.

BREAST OF CHICKEN IN RECEDING LANDSCAPE Renaissance landscapers used variations in size in order to build the illusion of depth into gardens and parks. You can use the same tricks when you're plating your food. Put low foods in the foreground of the plate, and build up height towards the back. Prop up your protein against a mountain of carbs.

Emergency Food Styling

When you simply must consume fast food on the go, use these simple designs inspired by exciting restaurant trends to elevate the humblest meal into a work of art.

TALL ORDER Mount burger on a carry out container; hold elements together with a plastic straw. Garnish with fries for added height.

SPA CUISINE Arrange low-calorie toppings in a sleek stripe. (Stash the patty in your purse for later.)

SLOW FOOD Make your own open-faced traffic light with burger, buns, and condiments.

FUSION CUISINE Create a Japanese flag by applying a thin layer of ketchup to a naked burger.

Drinking Inside the Box

The wine box is a good design with a bad image. The technology was introduced in Australia in 1965, where today, half of all wine is sold in a box. (Australians and New Zealanders also were early adapters of screw tops and plastic corks.) Wine boxes are popular in England, Italy, Sweden, Chile, and other countries worldwide, but not in the U.S., where the mystique of glass and cork weighs heavy—and where many consumers can't shake the product's frat house hangover.

Wherein lies the appeal of the wine box? First, it's cheap. Although premium wine boxes contain a higher grade of product than the giant cartons of swill served to underage drinkers, all boxed wines are sold as value products. (At the lower end of the wine spectrum, the glass bottle can cost more than the wine inside.) Second, the box is convenient. It's easy to open (no tools required), and the wine keeps for a month after it's been opened (no pressure to polish off a whole bottle at breakfast). The box's light weight lowers shipping costs and the associated use of petroleum as well as saving your own back. (Carry it to your local beach, pool, park, or preschool.) Finally, a box takes up less space than a bottle or jug, further conserving on shipping while saving shelf space.

Despite these compelling advantages, boxed wine needs a status boost. Manufacturers are rebranding the box, reaching out to a rising generation of consumers who may be willing to abandon the bottle in favor of convenience, ecology, and price (at least on weeknights). Animal themes (rabbits, fish, kangaroos) add a frisky rural finish to some of the new upscale cartons. Target has introduced a product called The Cube—a beverage that's proud of its box. DTOUR, developed by celebrity chef Daniel Boulud, cuts corners altogether by using a tall cardboard cylinder in place of a straight-sided carton.

Although these products are notching up the image of the box, none of them is a collector's item. The packaging is intended to hold liquids for no more than a year, after which point the plastic may start leaching into the wine. (Look for the use-by date.) Glass is far easier to recycle than either type of wine box, but the shipping costs still push the boxes ahead on the ecological balance sheet.

Hosts who are squeamish about putting a bladder on their holiday buffet or a juice box on their date-night dining table may be tempted to decant their boxed wine in the kitchen. Soon, however, the box might start feeling at home anywhere. **EL**

BLADDERS AND JUICE BOXES There are two kinds of wine box. The first, called "bag in a box," is also known as a "bladder" or "cask." It harkens back to the ancient technique of carrying wine in an animal skin. The other type, "asceptic packaging," is a resin-impregnated paper container equipped with an integral spout or screw top. Known by the trade name Tetra Pak, it is also called a "juice box," owing to its family relation to toddler-style juice bombs.

Table Shapes

The Vietnam Peace Conference of 1969 was preceded by widely publicized deliberations over table arrangements. The first plan centered around a great rectangular conference table, the kind of massive megalith familiar from peace talks and smorgasbords since the Middle Ages. Sovereigns, CEOs, and divorce lawyers alike favor the built-in formality of the long table, which establishes a clear head and forces warring parties to speak face-to-face while staying out of strangling reach. In search of a more democratic seating plan, the Vietnamese negotiators moved from rectangles to circles. Round tables, too, have a long history. In a legendary feat of furniture design, Merlin the magician created a round table for King Arthur and his knights, using the equal seating to reduce bickering and food fights among his top warriors. The Vietnam ambassadors went back and forth with various table arrangements, including squares, diamonds, and divided circles. In an Arthurian mood, they finally agreed on a big circle—bisected, however, by two small freestanding rectangular tables that split the meeting space into clear sides. (The talks failed anyway.)

Home life is war by other means, whether the problem is money in the bank, socks on the floor, or a dreaded bout of MFS (Me First Syndrome). The philosopher Hannah Arendt wrote in 1959, "To live together in the world means essentially that a world of things is between those who have it in common, as a table is located between those who sit around it; the world, like every in-between, relates and separates men at the same time." Tables bring people together, but they also help keep them apart, creating an open space and a neutral zone across which conflicting parties can search for peace.

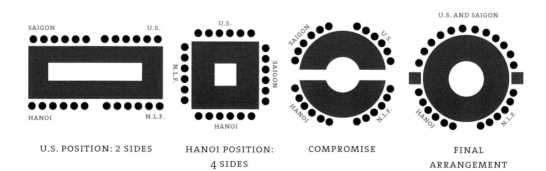

| U.S. POSITION: 2 SIDES | HANOI POSITION: 4 SIDES | COMPROMISE | FINAL ARRANGEMENT |

In the nineteenth century, dining rooms were associated with the man of the house. They often sported hunting themes, to honor the primacy of meat and the victorious return of the breadwinner at the dinner hour. Today, most dining rooms are designed to house a rectilinear table; the proverbial square meal sits well on a rectangle.

Circles, in contrast, have no natural focal point. They often nest in kitchens, where their small footprint and continuous circumference suits the morning traffic flow of bagels and backpacks. An oval table is just a parallelogram on drugs, but its soft lines can absorb additional chairs more easily than its angular counterparts.

Going against the grain of the traditional dining room, Ina Garten (aka "the Barefoot Contessa") prefers round tables for small dinner parties. "With six people, you can really get a conversation going. The ideal table for six or seven is a 48-inch round, because everyone is equally engaged in the conversation. If people are a little crowded, it feels even more intimate." For larger gatherings, she recommends

KNIGHTS OF THE ROUND TABLE Over the ages, artists have imagined King Arthur's table in various ways. Some represent it as a huge flat disk, while others depict an open donut shape. Our rendering is based on an illumination from a manuscript of Lancelot-Grail, completed in 1470. The circular arrangement is democratic in spirit, but Arthur got the best chair.

renting a few round tables (together with the necessary linens) from a party supplier.

A round table also makes a great office accessory. If you have your own office and your job draws a lot of face time, try squeezing a small round table into a front corner. People won't even know why they're smiling, but the circular setting can really break the ice, whether you're speaking with an important client or a testy colleague. Retreat behind your big desk to stake out a safe position.

Small circles may be true conversation pieces, but the ungainly disks favored by banquet halls are weapons of mass construction. The 72-inch round (standard fare at weddings and galas) conserves real estate and allows ten to twelve guests to sit together. Alas, its fold-out acreage seems destined to hold you hostage to the old guy with the hearing aid to your right, leaving the hipsters on the opposite side of the table to wink and sparkle faintly across a battlefield of glassware and super-sized flora.

Whether your table is shaped like an amoeba or a boomerang, the search for mealtime order remains a holy grail in most households. Assigned seating quietly sets household order on the firm footing that only four legs or a sturdy pedestal can provide. The reigning adults of the household often have better conversations if they occupy two corner seats, an arrangement that maps a happy diagonal between side-by-side cuddling and face-to-face discussion.

Everyone should clear his own plate. Or else it's war. JL

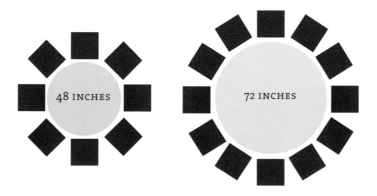

Talk to anyone you like

Chained to your
immediate neighbors

Nice Legs

When shopping for a table, pay attention to the legs. The number of people that can sit at a table is affected not only by the size of the tabletop, but by the placement of the legs. Generally, legs that are set in from the edge are more accommodating to chairs, in contrast with legs pushed out to the perimeter.

MÉNAGE À TROIS Jean Prouvé's 28-inch round Gueridon table, designed c. 1946, is scaled for intimate conversations. The sexily splayed legs make it awkward to fit more than three chairs around the table, although the circumference would easily seat four.

URBAN RENEWAL Eero Saarinen's pedestal tables, designed in 1956, keep table legs completely out of the way. Saarinen explained, "The underside of typical chairs and tables makes a confusing, unrestful world. I wanted to clear up the slum of legs."

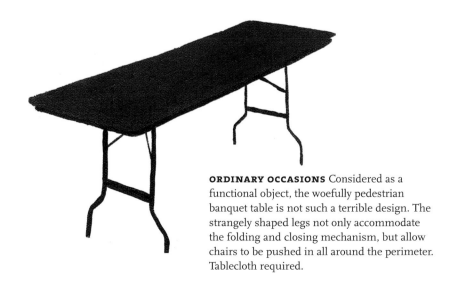

ORDINARY OCCASIONS Considered as a functional object, the woefully pedestrian banquet table is not such a terrible design. The strangely shaped legs not only accommodate the folding and closing mechanism, but allow chairs to be pushed in all around the perimeter. Tablecloth required.

PLACE CARDS Some hosts feel that place cards are too fussy, formal, or controlling for a casual dinner party, yet using this simple planning tool can curb the chaos that erupts as your guests transition from cocktail hour to the dinner table.

HANDMADE *A place card need not be elaborate—have your kids make them with Sharpies and index cards, or write them yourself on a piece of origami paper or any small slip of paper or cardstock. These were penned on vintage rolodex cards by Ruby, age 9.*

ENTERTAINING: THE SPEED-DATING WAY Speed-dating was invented in order to maximize on people's intuitive sense of connection (or disconnection) with each other and to cut down on wasted steaks. The technique was invented by Aish HaTorah, an outreach group whose contribution to a Jewish tomorrow was sealed when they figured out how to cut the ancient art of matchmaking to the bare minimum: gather a group of singles; allow them to talk for as little as three minutes; then ring the bell and make them move on to the next candidate.

Since its inception in Beverly Hills in 1998, speed-dating has not only gone secular; it has also migrated to other forms of social interaction. In London, the Commission for Architecture and the Built Environment decided to apply the principles of speed-dating to match skittish architects with bottom-line developers. The two groups were corralled into a banquet hall, where they proceeded to rotate through their pitches in order to find common ground without Power Points or power lunches.

Speed-dating is to the blind date what the cocktail party is to the formal dinner. An extended meal around a shared table can lock you and your guests into a miserable staring contest where the only out is an emergency call from the baby sitter (just set your cell on alarm). At a cocktail party, however, guests can circulate freely until they find a conversation that sticks. Potlucks and buffets incorporate dinner into the evening without forcing familiarity over too many hours. If you want the full orchestral rhythm of a classic dinner party without the claustrophobia, try moving into another room for dessert.

SEATING CHART

Place your guests carefully to generate energy, buzz, and even mischief. Party politics? Global swarming? Some really foul play?

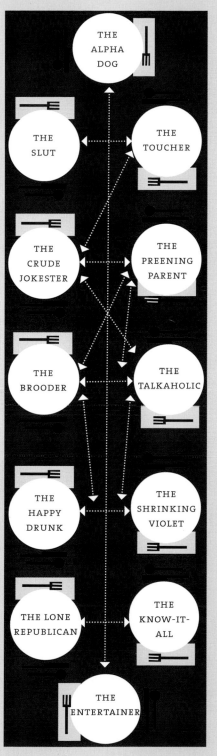

Put someone capable of leadership at the head of the table. It could be the host, or the oldest person in the room, or an honored guest.

Put the sex-obsessed people together, but use furniture to separate the truly dangerous ones.

Some parents bring their kids everywhere—even when the little darlings are at home with a sitter.

Use the crude jokester and the preening parent to keep the talkaholic from taking over. These two can be counted on to keep the conversation coming back to teething, nursery decor, and non-reproductive sex.

Introspective guests provide acoustic insulation between the loudmouths.

Give the Op-Ed expert a worthy opponent.

Placing your most socially gifted guest at one head of the table can keep the evening in motion.

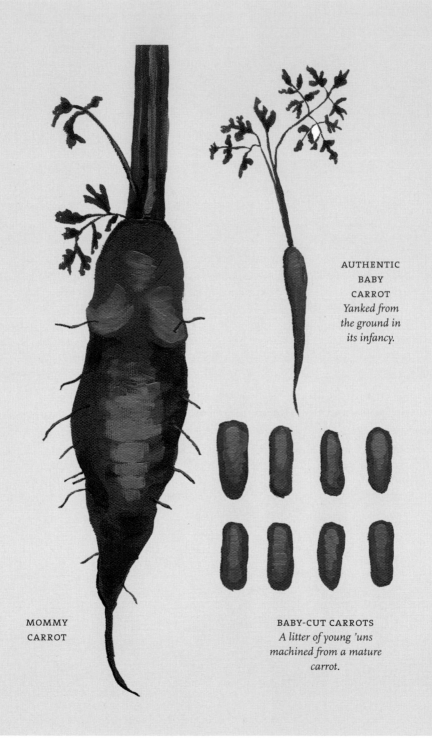

AUTHENTIC
BABY
CARROT
*Yanked from
the ground in
its infancy.*

MOMMY
CARROT

BABY-CUT CARROTS
*A litter of young 'uns
machined from a mature
carrot.*

MOMMY, WHERE DO BABY CARROTS COME FROM?

There they sit, bag after bag of clean, tiny, perfectly shaped carrots, waiting on the produce shelf for some family to take them home. Where do they come from, these paragons of vegetal perfection?

Baby carrots are made, not born. Perfectly uniform in size and, like true newborns, always naked, these stubby infants are actually milled out of the deformed bodies of adult carrots too bent out of shape to line up nicely in the long plastic body bags that have housed the traditional "cello carrots" since the 1950s.

The baby carrot as we know it is the brainchild of California farmer Mike Yurosek. Watching as much as 70 percent of his carrot crop go into the waste heap of his Bakersfield packing plant, Yurosek figured out how to factory-whittle the ungainly rejects into the orange missiles that we now call "baby carrots." Yurosek used a commercial green bean cutter to cut the adult carrot into "babies." Then he used an industrial potato peeler to remove the skin and extra flesh.

Presto—the Baby Carrot, which now dominates supermarket carrot sales. Its arrival has cut down agricultural waste, but it has added more packaging, along with extra cost to the consumer. Baby carrots like to congregate in children's lunch boxes—where, however, they are often delivered stillborn straight to the trash.

Though reengineered for sweetness, these factory-milled beta-bullets lack the fresh sheen and earthy bite of a full-sized, freshly peeled carrot. In modern snack-bag households, the sudden appearance of an adult carrot can produce shock and awe, along with a genuine flavor burst in soups, salads, and sides. **J L**

CARROT COINAGE *In 1989, stores bought cello carrots (cleaned carrots packed in a bag) for 10 cents a bag and sold them for 17 cents. A comparable bag of babies cost the store 50 cents, and could be sold for a dollar.*

Gateway Vegetables

Could a child you know be eating more
vegetables than you think?

CHIPS AND SALSA Like pizza sauce and ketchup, salsa is a nutrient-rich condiment that sneaks past the radar of many veggie-adverse kids. It is commonly consumed, of course, with corn chips.

CORN Many kids will eat corn on the cob, corn muffins, or canned corn, especially when bribed with a (corn-sweetened) dessert or beverage. Many, however, draw the line at corned beef, as well as corny jokes like this one. Nutritionally, corn is a junk starch, but the unprocessed kernels do introduce another texture into children's diets. And bowel movements.

FRIES Technically speaking, a potato is a root vegetable, but unlike its virtuous cousins the beet, the carrot, and the turnip, it has dubious nutritional value beyond its heavy carbo load. Deep fry it and it's even more irresistible.

KETCHUP Although Ronald Reagan got a lot of bad press for counting ketchup as a school-lunch vegetable, the beloved condiment contains Vitamin C, the antioxidant lycopene, and even a little protein.

CHICKEN FINGERS Is fried chicken really corn? Food critic Michael Pollan argues that a creature who is fed only corn ends up being more corn on the lunch tray.

Novelty Food Formats

Children could be more willing to sample strange new foods, including green ones, if they were presented with a sense of fun and fanfare.

BROCCOLI IN A TUBE Squirtable foods, although banned from some preschool lunchrooms, provide diverse pleasures. Small children enjoy sucking food from the packaging as well as making rude sounds with it or simply shooting the contents across the room.

BROCCOLI IN A BOX Boxed beverages are modular and spoil-proof—but not spill-proof. Warning: Contents are projectile when box is squeezed.

BROCCOLI NUGGETS Nearly any menu item transforms into an appealing entertainment once it has been pulverized, mixed with corn meal, molded into a simple iconic shape, and deep fried.

BROCCOLI ON A STICK Even the most unadorned food item becomes a festive treat when impaled on a stick.

Baby Lettuce

Designer leaves first appeared as a gourmet product for yuppies (in open bins) and then as a convenience item for working mothers (in plastic bags). The tender leaves, tasty when fresh, are prone to early rot, especially when confined in plastic. A few rotten leaves can stink up the whole bag. If that's not enough to turn you off, think about this: baby lettuces, like spinach leaves, are washed in great promiscuous vats along with thousands of other lettuces, a situation that could leave baby lettuce more prone to bacterial contamination. Cut tissues may further nourish bacterial growth, contributing to that California classic, *pasta e coli*.

SELL-BY DATE
*Bagging
encourages
extended shelf
life.*

INCUBATOR
*Leaves gathered
from multiple
plants share
germs.*

TENDER IS
THE BLIGHT
*Infant leaves
decay quickly,
and cut ends
encourage rot.*

DESIGNER LEAVES
*Lettuce growers add hard, bitter leaves such
as radicchio and frisee (aka "pubes") not
because people love to eat them, but because
they help air circulate in the bag.*

OLD SOCK FACTOR
*Bag traps air, moisture,
and rank smells.*

MAIDENHEAD
Tender inner leaves nestle together intact.

SELF-COOLING
Open structure of lettuce head encourages ventilation.

BETTER THAN SOAP
Outer leaves protect interior from exposure to bacteria carried by other lettuces.

BODY ARMOR
Outer leaves take the hit from rough handling.

ROMAINE

ICEBERG Lettuce is an ancient food plant with its roots in the Mediterranean. The "crisphead" type (of which iceberg is the most prevalant variety) was engineered to resist disease and to permit shipping. Iceberg got its name when it began being trucked on ice from California to other parts of the United States. With its remarkably high water content, iceberg is low on nutrients; it has only 300 mgs of vitamin A per 100 grams, as compared to 2,600 in romaine lettuce.

Have You Ever Tried Chicken?

Boneless breast of chicken is everywhere. It's cheap. It requires minimal preparation. It cooks quickly. This ubiquitous protein, however, is more than a convenience. It represents the abstraction of flesh from fowl, of animal protein from its origins in a living creature. The very phrase "white meat" evokes the purity of an angel, forever divorced from prior scenes of life or death. Be gone, skin—and with it, all memory of fat and feather. Rest in peace, bones: and with them, all remains of frame and structure. Farewell, wings—and with them, all fantasy of flight, all glimpse of possible gesture.

Boneless chicken painlessly initiates children into the world of meat-eating. Many members of this newest generation, increasingly attuned to the anguish of penguins and polar bears, will eat meat only under conditions of extreme mystification. Salads, burritos, pastas, and pizza are increasingly colonized by bits of bird. Chicken has become both main course and condiment, a ubiquitous check-builder that translates vegetarian offerings from around the world into square meals worthy to grace the American table.

According to historian Roger Horowitz, chicken gained ground after World War II, thanks to new hybrids and heads-off, no-feet packaging. Yet marketers kept encountering "chicken fatigue" in the consumers they surveyed. Chicken, it turned out—even the new, better, bigger chicken—was always . . . chicken. In 1962, more than 90 percent of chickens were sold whole: too much for two people, marketers learned, but not enough for a large family. Pork and beef, on the other hand, came in many cuts and price points (bacon, steak, ribs; bologna, dogs, rinds). Tyson introduced the chicken nugget, and Perdue brought us branding, selling cut-up birds that were dated, labeled, and priced right in the processing plant. "Product differentiation" broke the fatigue, and chicken became king.

The boneless breast was another innovation. In the 1970s, its blankness invited cooks to add something vaguely French—a dab of Dijon, a whiff of curry, or a pinch of dried tarragon. Today, chicken chunks are unceremoniously grilled, baked, poached, or even boiled before landing naked atop a rice bowl or salad plate.

Although chicken is America's favorite meat, consumers rank taste last among the bird's major selling points (which include "versatility," "convenience," and "economy," making chicken the ultimate cheap date). Marketers have developed several branding hooks in an effort to make chicken sexier. "Organic" and "free range" refer to specific agricultural practices, while "kosher" and "halal" are ritual forms of slaughter. Although all chickens are "natural" and "farm-raised," the label suggests improved wholesomeness.

Watch out for "enhanced" chicken. This processing technique injects the meat with a solution of water, salt, and phosphates. The motive isn't to pump up the bird's purchase weight, though: these fowl breast enhancements compensate for tissue damage caused by breeding chickens for all that extra white meat. Perhaps the best way to combat chicken fatigue is not with saline solution, but with tofu, seafood, chickenless Caesar, beans, and the occasional whole bird. JL

Tastes like rattlesnake

Designer Chicken: Future Trends

BLANCMANGE Medieval cooks invented *blancmange* ("white food"), a gelatinous pudding made from chicken, milk, ground almonds, rice, and sugar. Quivering somewhere between a dessert and a slime mold, blancmange was also called, simply, "shape." Today, scientists are working on the ultimate *blancmange*: edible tissue cultured directly from muscle stem cells of chickens, turkeys, pigs, and cows. (Experiments have also been performed on rats—white ones, we hope!) Grown in thin sheets, the technique would yield the raw matter for processed foods, such as nuggets and sausage, but not for "highly structured meats, such as steaks." Let alone chicken feet.

WHITER MEAT "Dark" meat gets its color from myoglobin, a protein that provides oxygen to cells during exercise. Myoglobin collects in the legs because that's where all the action is. Poultry scientist Mirko Betti, who fled his native Italy for the blander zones of Alberta, Canada, has invented a way to purge myoglobin from chicken, reducing the tasty thighs and legs—the bird's last flavor reserves—into a pale protein mush suitable for shaping into nuggets and loafs.

WILD CHICKENS OF HAWAII Parts of Hawaii are infested with feral chickens. Some descended from live cargo brought by the first settlers to Hawaii in 500 CE; others hail from fighting roosters that accompanied Filipino laborers in the early twentieth century. Striving to keep up with their domestic cousins, the wild chickens of Hawaii hang out around supermarket parking lots looking for corn-based snacks. Are they pests? Or the next big food craze for mainlanders itching for exotic bird flesh?

WARNING: GRAPHIC CONTENT

D.I.Y. BRANDING *People are making and sharing their own goods, from fruits and veggies to books and media.*

GARAGE BRANDING

Pamphlets, press kits, and Post-its. Mugs, matchbooks, and magnets. The tools and trinkets of branding are everywhere. And they don't just say "Starbucks" or "Apple" anymore. They read "Emma's Hand-knit Laptop Sleeves" or "Welcome to Bob and Bill's Wedding" or "Free: Soviet jewelry."

Brands used to belong to big corporations, who could hire ad agencies to design marketing campaigns and blast them through mainstream media channels. Now, thanks to the rise of desktop publishing, Internet marketplaces, and print-on-demand services, branding has gone local. Companies like CaféPress make it easy and affordable to imprint almost anything with a scan of your ex-husband's Viagra prescription. Meanwhile, it's not just Mom and Pop's dry cleaning business that's sporting some snappy new graphics. Gothic Gertrude is pushing her bespoke dog sweaters on Etsy.com, while Slacker Sam is hawking his artisanal ring tones through his file-sharing networks. In the brave new world of D.I.Y. branding, really small businesses are selling their stuff and their services, along with their personalities and their politics, using widely available digital tools. (Make it in Photoshop. Share it on Facebook. Take orders with Paypal.)

Branding doesn't just belong to business, though. Any group with a goal, whether it's raising money for penguin relief or barking the virtues of puggles, can use design to make connections and raise consciousness. Non-profits, once distinguished by tone-deaf form letters, now have access to clean information graphics and sophisticated marketing tools. So do the in-house organizers of weddings, children's parties, sewing circles, and campaigns for class president.

For the last few decades, universities have engaged in top-down, Helvetica-heavy branding programs. If Corporate U has opted for bland neutrality along with bottom-line reasoning, smaller sectors on college campuses are using design for more ad-hoc, expressive forms of branding. Students packaging their research papers, teachers promoting new seminars, and techie librarians announcing the latest database are using graphic design to reshape and revitalize campus communications, from the ground up.

Since the 1950s, when Florida companies began putting resort names and Disney characters on t-shirts, the simple tee has been a corporate message board. It has also offered a blank slate for D.I.Y. fashion and sub-cultural branding. Small print runs at local silk screen shops have long allowed bands and clubs to tune their image and build their bases. Iron-on transfers, fabric paints, and permanent markers have generated Extra-Small and one-of-a-kind t-shirt batching. Threadless.com, a print-on-demand t-shirt enterprise, has built its brand out of the D.I.Y. efforts of its users, whose uploads, downloads, and ranking systems provide both the retail catalog and the branding ambience of the site.

Whether it's for business, pleasure, or just to save the world, a little good design can go a long way in building group morale and a sense of belonging. Turn folders into press kits using cheap materials from the local office mart. (Branding addicts may quickly graduate, though, to online purveyors of wholesale labels, exotic papers, and blank mouse pads.) "Pink ribbon" your activities by finding a cheap, memorable icon for your cause. (Websites and blogs are easy to customize for specific events or business ventures.)

Meanwhile, big brands keep getting bigger. Their modus operandi, however, has become increasingly two-way. Early marketers focused on shaping consumer desire. After World War II, market researchers began to use surveys in order to understand consumer wants. Still, the brand itself was a one-way communiqué that aimed to deliver desires back to the buyer in the form of new products. In the last decade, businesses have shifted their focus from sending ads out into the world to managing the brand's social life once it gets there. The migration of a brand from cars or skateboards to t-shirts and decals, parties and clubs, link lists and tag lines, and even jokes and parodies helps morph the meaning and seal the success of a brand. The use of "real" models and street photography by purveyors like Benneton, American Apparel, and Heineken puts the consumer directly into the branded scene. Starbucks has gone global in part because its most iconic customers want to write novels at its tables. Even hostile action—as when Apple users organized in order to protest the lowering of the iPhone's price—ultimately builds brand equity. Brandom has become a version of fandom.

The downside of all this branding is that contemporary social worlds are increasingly shaped by retail trends, even or especially when the actions of consumers are building the brands. The upside is that creative consumers are learning a few tricks from the world of marketing. D.I.Y. often seems caught between co-opt and opt-out—

between the appropriation of homegrown styles by the mass-marketing machine over there on the right, and the no-logo call to retreat from consumerism altogether, way out on the left. There is, however, a middle way. By providing tools and creating new models and markets for social and economic entrepreneurship, D.I.Y. is charting new entrances into the general economy for micro-businesses and nonprofits that want to stay small while paying at least some of bills.

But wait. Too much branding, whether it's at the corporate café or on CaféPress, may be going the way of matchy-matchy in decorating circles. If "coolness" equals successful resistance to consumer culture, than the coolest brand may be the one that doesn't look or feel like a brand at all. The new trend among design-driven businesses is to strip away the logos and run on pure taste-making and a sense of curatorial exactitude. Heralding from Japan, MUJI is a no-brand brand that creates low-cost, high-value products ranging from notebooks to home furnishings. Their offerings are simple, austere, anonymous—and magnificently beautiful. Rob Forbes, the founder of the modernist furniture empire, Design Within Reach, has now launched Studio Forbes, a blog, gallery, and online store whose values are more inquisitive than acquisitive, more research than retail.

Maybe you don't need a logo—just a clear sense of your own direction in the labyrinth of signs—and a few good fonts. **JL**

MUJI: MATTRESS WITH LEGS *The company seeks to simplify basic products by eliminating unnecessary elements. Why purchase a separate bed frame, headboard, and box spring when you can buy a mattress with legs? This anonymous approach defines the brand.*

Name-Storming

A good name nails the essence of an event or group. It's also a sequence of letterforms that may lead to a logotype. The name is the living link between the brand (the idea, mood, and ambience of a product) and the logo (the visual representation of the brand). But how to find a name that will stick?

Brainstorming was invented in 1953 by Alex Osborn, an advertising executive and author of the book *Applied Imagination*. Osborn had a military metaphor in mind: to "brainstorm" is to attack a problem from numerous directions with the combined force of a group of minds. Today, we often think of a "brainstorm" as any frenzied outpouring of ideas, mostly bad ones, intended to uncover a few useful gems. Brainstorming externalizes the thought process. Capturing ideas frees the mind to move on to the next notion as well as stimulating further thought by presenting the eye with multiple concepts to leap off from.

Brainstorming Principles
1. More is more. (Generate lots of ideas.)
2. Edit later. (Don't reject ideas until you've got a pile of them.)
3. Weird is wonderful. (Let your mind wander.)
4. Hyphenate and hybridize. (Combine good ideas into better ones.)

Brainstorming Steps for Groups
1. Appoint a moderator.
2. Define the problem clearly.
3. Record all ideas without ranking them.
4. Set a time limit. (Participants will be more active when they know the exercise will be short.)
5. Rank ideas at the end of the gathering period.

Name-Storming Session for a Progressive Bake Sale

Sweets for the Sweet:
Bake Sale for Literacy

~~Business as Usual:~~
Baking a Better Future

Half-Baked:
Fruit and Cookies for a Sweeter Tomorrow

Baker's Dozen:
Neighbors against Hunger

Cupcakes for Change

Cookie Revolution

Food Fight
(A Militant Bake Sale)

Ice Cream Socialism

Donuts for Democracy

The Bread Brigade

Rice Cake Rally

Juice for Justice

Peace-za Party

BAKE SALES ARE BACK Even a bake sale can have a brand. A graphic program (consistent colors, fonts, and sprinkles) can be applied not only to flyers and table signs, but also to the food itself. "Icing printers" allow you to transfer complex designs directly to a sheet cake (service available at most grocery store bakeries). In 2008, MoveOn.org used social media to host thousands of bake sales across America to support progressive campaigns in the coming election; tables were laden with pamphlets as well as snacks. Children took an active role in what was for many their first real election. Cake designed by Hannah Reinhard, age 12; drawing inspired by Shepard Fairy.

Business Cards

Business cards aren't just for business. These handy little printed pieces are upstaging postcards and club flyers as a sleeker, leaner way to promote products and events. Use them for party invitations, announcements, price tags, gift tags, save-the-date cards, place cards, and calling cards as well as a means to deliver your contact info to potential employers, clients, and love interests.

1-800-GOT-FISH	LICENSED TO KILL
SAMURAI SUSHI CHEF	
PO BOX 1760	MADISON, WS 21210

Back in the day, a typical business card featured a stiff line of type stuck in each corner with a name plopped in the middle. Today, ugly templates supplied by online printing services are the norm. Pick your business (beauty shop, pet care, escort service), and there's a color-drenched, fully illustrated template waiting out there for you.

Yet anyone with basic software skills (Photoshop, Illustrator, InDesign, Quark, or even a standard word processor) can set up a unique design and print cards online or with a desktop printer. Skip the templates (or stick to the simple ones) and express your own point of view.

Samurai Sushi Chef	**Samurai Sushi Chef** 1-800-GOT-FISH Licensed to kill	**Samurai Sushi Chef** 1-800-GOT-FISH Licensed to kill
Samurai Sushi Chef		

Most online services use digital printing, a four-color process like that used on a desktop ink jet printer. Digital printing lets you use as many colors as you want. Rather than pull out the whole Crayola box, combine just a few colors to create emphasis. Experiment with various fonts as well as with different colors for your text and background.

Pictures are powerful, but text is tough to read on top of a busy background. If you are an artist, photographer, or craftista, consider putting a full-bleed image of your work on the back of your card instead of on the front; the image and text won't have to compete, and your business card will become a miniature portfolio piece. **EL**

Design Your Own Modern Business Card in 6 Easy Steps

Samurai Sushi Chef
1-800-GOT-FISH
PO box 1760
Madison, WS 21210

Available for weddings,
bar mitzvahs, and ritual
suicides.

1. Arrange type in simple blocks, all one size. Decide exactly what information to include.

Samurai Sushi Chef   1-800-GOT-FISH
PO box 1760
Madison, WS 21210

Available for weddings,
bar mitzvahs, and ritual
suicides.

2. Use spatial arrangement to create emphasis. (The most important element doesn't have to go in the middle.)

Samurai Sushi Chef   1-800-GOT-FISH
PO box 1760
Madison, WS 21210

*Available for weddings,
bar mitzvahs, and ritual
suicides.*

3. Change the size, weight, color, or font of key elements; add logo if desired.

4. Use color to create drama and bring further attention to important information.

5. Try alternate designs using the same elements.

6. Become obsessed. Lose mind over limitless possibilities. Choose a design. Regain sanity.

EAT FONTS

Everybody who uses a computer knows something about fonts. It didn't used to be that way—typefaces were once the exclusive domain of professional designers. Today, Times Roman and Helvetica are ubiquitous, and tens of thousands of other fonts are available for use by anyone who can buy the software. How is even the most eager font nerd supposed to make sense of these endless variations?

Students in my basic typography courses often start the semester with a question like this: "When will we learn what typefaces *mean*? You know, like, what font should we use for a particular job?"

Their eager faces cloud with disappointment at my cold reply: "Most typefaces don't mean anything at all."

As I see it, the vast and overwhelming world of fonts can be divided into two basic categories: coffee and donuts. Coffee is dark, acidic, and invigorating. Donuts are soft, sweet, and sticky, causing a brief elevation in mood quickly followed by gas and low-grade depression.

Certain typefaces aim to be meaningful: wedding scripts, fake neon, distressed "garage fonts" of various sorts, and letters built from twigs, flames, or soccer balls. Most typefaces, however, are abstract, aiming only to express the basic shapes of the alphabet in a distinctive and consistent way. End of story. Classical serif typefaces like Garamond and Caslon as well as modern sans serifs like Helvetica and Univers are, essentially, abstract.

Once in a while, a designer uses letterforms to brilliantly mirror the content at hand. The logotype for Dunkin' Donuts, designed in the 1970s, still holds strong today as an indelible signifier of deep-fried, sugar-glazed bakery treats. The logo's pudgy, rounded letterforms are packed together in a neat rectangle, like donuts in a box. The Tootsie Roll logotype is another rare instance of this form/content synergy. It employs Oswald Cooper's eponymous 1930s typeface Cooper Black (also used extensively on t-shirts in the 1970s). A few seductive, sugar-loaded examples like these can send a designer down a lifelong search for meaningful typography.

Most logotypes bear no resemblance whatsoever to their content, yet they nonetheless become linked in our minds with a company or product—even when the letterforms themselves are not only abstract, but utterly commonplace. The letters in the Starbucks logo are similar to those in Futura, a geometric typeface designed in Germany in the 1920s, at the time of the Bauhaus. Futura, one of the world's most widely used typefaces, appears today in hundreds of corporate logotypes. The Starbucks logo also resembles Freight Sans, a font designed by Joshua Darden in 2005. At first glance, the typefaces shown below look similar, yet designers learn to tell them apart by studying details such as the letter *R*.

STARBUCKS
GILL SANS

STARBUCKS
FUTURA

STARBUCKS
HELVETICA

STARBUCKS
FREIGHT SANS

A well-designed font is like a prize-winning potato. Most people can't tell one potato from another. But potato experts surely can, as demonstrated each August at agricultural fairs around the land. The state or county fair is a late-summer rite that features carnival rides, cotton candy, pregnant cows, and quiet air-conditioned halls filled with perfect vegetables. There, displayed on tier after tier of shelving, sit dozens of carrots, onions, peppers, and potatoes, proudly arrayed on ruffled paper plates. To me, a potato is just a potato. I can't see what makes one brown-eyed spud different from the next. Yet the judges will come through and endow one proud platter of tubers with a bright blue ribbon.

Graphic designers bring that same appreciation to letterforms. Typefaces don't need to be fancy or original to do their job. A few basic fonts are all you need to create beautiful and distinctive publications, from reports and proposals to flyers, invitations, bomb threats, and books of poetry. If fancy fonts are important to you, try washing one down with a brisk cup of coffee on the side. **EL**

SMOOTH
sexy spuds

SPECIES: **GARAMOND**

ORIGIN: *France, 1500s; Claude Garamond*

HABITAT: *This hardy Renaissance font thrives in books of prose or poetry.*

DISTINCTIVE MARKINGS: *Pretty but tough, these letters are built with sturdy calligraphic strokes.*

HOT
crispy fries

SPECIES: **GILL SANS**

ORIGIN: *England, 1928; Eric Gill*

HABITAT: *Britain's most popular sans serif typeface, it is known as the Helvetica of the U.K.*

DISTINCTIVE MARKINGS: *Plain and simple but not severe.*

Proud *plump*
POTATOES

SPECIES: **CASLON**

ORIGIN: *England, 1734–70; William Caslon*

HABITAT: *Caslon was popular during the American Revolution; use it for drafting declarations, constitutions, and whatnot.*

DISTINCTIVE MARKINGS: *Slim, sharp serifs and upright forms.*

RIPE ROUND
rhizomes

SPECIES: **FUTURA**

ORIGIN: *Germany, 1927; Paul Renner*

HABITAT: *This strict geometric typeface, designed in the Bauhaus era, is used in logos, books, signage, and info graphics around the world.*

DISTINCTIVE MARKINGS: *Look for the round O and the pointy Ms and Ns.*

blunt *bland*
BLOBS

SPECIES: **TIMES ROMAN / TIMES NEW ROMAN**

ORIGIN: *England, 1931; Stanley Morison*

HABITAT: *Created for a London newspaper, Times Roman became the ubiquitous font of desktop publishing in the 1980s.*

DISTINCTIVE MARKNGS: *Its pinched, narrow body was designed to save space on cheap newsprint. Avoid it when you want to make your publications different from everyone else's.*

sleek *salty*
STARCH

SPECIES: **HELVETICA**

ORIGIN: *Switzerland, 1957; Max Miedinger*

HABITAT: *Helvetica is at home absolutely everywhere: banks, airports, trendy t-shirts, and New York City garbage trucks.*

DISTINCTIVE MARKINGS: *The teardrop bowl of the lowercase A and the oddly curved leg of the uppercase R are signature features of this classic Swiss typeface.*

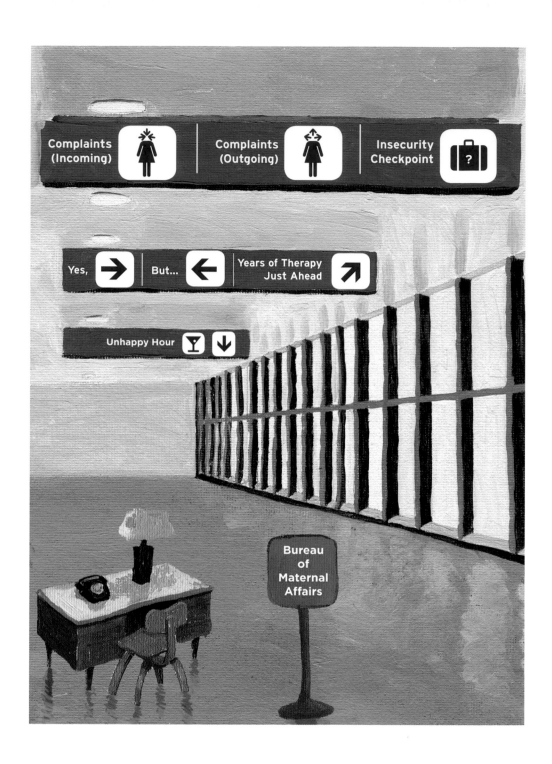

NO EXIT *What if a signage system could guide us through our interpersonal landscapes?*

SIGNS OF FAILURE

A prominent graphic designer once created elegant interior signs for a concert hall, pointing the way to the gift shop, the restrooms, the auditorium, and more. The architect and the client loved the signs because they were set into the walls flush with the outer surface—no ugly plaques or panels were sticking out and casting shadows. Unfortunately, the signs were so discreet they almost disappeared. Many people weren't noticing them, so the institution erected free-standing stanchions around the building, emblazoned with the same text that was so subtly embedded in the walls behind them.

"Signage" is a design specialty devoted to guiding people through airports, hospitals, schools, and other public places. In a major building project, a signage specialist works to brand the building as well as create room markers and directional signs designed to lead users where they want to go. Signs have attitude and personality. They can command, scold, welcome, or resassure. Laws governing the number, placement, size, and visual treatment of signs help keep everyone moving smoothly, including people with disabilities.

Despite all of the money and expertise directed at signage, evidence of confusion can be observed in nearly any sparkling new edifice or renovated office suite. Every time you see a piece of poster board propped in a window or a sheet of office paper duct-taped to a desk or door, you are witnessing signs of failure—the failure to anticipate how people will actually use a space.

A well-designed building needs fewer signs than a poorly designed one. The front door looks like an entrance, and the bathroom is located where you might expect to find it. (In most restaurants, you can locate the restrooms without following an elaborate trail of arrows.) Receptionists and security staff are on the front lines of signage failure, forced to show the hordes of clueless wanderers where to find the elevator, the gift shop, or the ninth circle of hell. These harried gatekeepers often get exasperated with the public, yet the real object of their irritation should be the designers and middle managers responsible for their building's signs and layout. Offered on the following pages are field notes on signage failure and signage solutions. EL

An Archaeology of Signage

The image shown at right is reconstructed from a real office foyer at a large state university. Native informants (office workers at the school) explained to us the history of the three distinct phases of signage found on the site, all of which remain fully intact today. Thus preserved in time is an instructive tale of bureaucratic process, institutional pride, and fearless individual initiative. Look closely at your own environment, and you will see such stories all around you.

THE SITE The scene of our inquiry is the entrance area shared by two related yet distinct academic departments within the university. One department is called "Art History and Archaeology," while the other is the "Department of Art." The former is devoted to the scholarly study of civilization and its artifacts, while the latter is dedicated to hands-on studio practice.

PHASE ONE: THE PLASTICUS PLAQUE PERIOD Sometime in the 1980s, a campus-wide signage program was implemented by the Facilities division, who needed to assign official room numbers to every area of the school in order to respond to service calls. Made from modules of beige plastic, the plaques appear to have been ordered from a standard catalog—perhaps the same one from which Facilities orders toilet paper and floor polish. Placed low on the wall, these signs were commonly ignored by students and visitors, who tended to walk through the wrong door and then ask the staff inside where the hell they were.

PHASE TWO: THE BLACK-AND-WHITE PERIOD Towards the end of the twentieth century, the Chair of the Department of Art decided that "professional" signage was needed. Thus he decreed that two elegant black placards be installed above the doors, featuring large, classical lettering. Students and visitors ignored these signs as well.

PHASE THREE: THE DO-IT-YOURSELF PERIOD Finally, a courageous staff member, tired of rerouting confused persons, took matters into her own hands. She made a sign out of laminated office paper and backed it up with sheets of colored card stock for dramatic emphasis. Key to the success of this homely yet functional new sign are the in-your-face placement, the hard-to-miss arrows, and the simplified text (reworded to reflect the way students, faculty, and staff actually refer to the two departments). The new sign is not pretty, but it gets people where they need to go. Staff on the ground, forced to deal with confused folk on a day-to-day basis, are often inspired to produce low-tech but effective signs.

MISGUIDED: *Three epochs in the life of a signage program*

Guerilla Signage Tactics

Among the most ubiquitous homemade signs are those in women's bathrooms imploring us not to flush sanitary pads and tampons down the toilet. I often used to wonder, while sitting there doing my business in a public lavatory, "Who is it that actually does flush their monthlies down the toilet, causing needless hassle to shopkeepers and maintenance crews around the land? Don't we all know better by now?" Then, one weekend the topic somehow came up with a female guest at my house. "Oh," she said, "I always flush tampons down the toilet, just not pads." Now I know the truth; all those signs—scrawled in Sharpie or computer-printed in Times New Roman—are for her.

When you need to discourage people from bumping their heads, missing their step, or peeing in your pool, what you need is a sign. Here are some tips on making temporary signs that look good and communicate clearly and calmly.

PLEASE DO NOT FLUSH SANITARY PADS, TAMPONS, PAPER TOWELS, CHEESE BURGERS, HOT DOGS, OR YESTERDAY'S NEWSPAPER DOWN THE TOILET.

HUGE ALL CAPS *(you are crazy)*

Please do not flush sanitary pads, tampons, paper towels, cheese burgers, hot dogs, or yesterday's newspaper down the toilet.

MODERATELY-SIZED UPPER AND LOWER CASE *(you are in control)*

TYPOGRAPHY Be polite. You may be angry, disappointed, or ready to shoot the next clueless person who tries to flush their September *Vogue* down your toilet, but yelling at these people won't make them behave better. Text written in all-capital letters makes you look frantic and out of control; try upper and lower case for a tone of confident, relaxed authority.

SIZE Homemade signs are usually printed on full sheets of 8.5-x-11-inch paper, because that's what comes out of your office printer. But many signs will work just fine printed on half a sheet of paper or even less. Take a seat in your local bathroom stall. A bold sans serif typeface such as Helvetica will be highly legible from a short distance in sizes ranging from 14 to 18 points.

Customer Care Center
Closed for breakfast, lunch, inventory, or staff meetings during all hours of operation. Please don't come back later.

Customer Care Center
Closed for breakfast, lunch, inventory, or staff meetings during all hours of operation. Please don't come back later.

MASKING TAPE *(you're fired)*   PICTURE FRAME *(you're hired)*

Save the world.
Turn out the lights.

TINY SIGN *laminated with packing tape. This handy technique also works well for labeling storage bins.*

MAKING AND INSTALLING SIGNS Plain paper signs are adequate in an emergency, but they hold up poorly over time. To create a more permanent sign, put your printout in a simple picture frame (very nice), mount it to foam bord (kind of nice), or laminate it with plastic (ugly, but you can wash it). Tiny signs can be laminated with clear packing tape.

Signs are generally installed at eye level. Of course, eye levels vary from person to person; the standard dimension used in the United States is sixty inches from the floor, which accommodates people in wheel chairs. Sign companies can make many kinds of signs for you, from large-scale banners to adhesive vinyl letters and plaques in braille with raised text. For major projects, work with a professional designer—but stay involved, very involved.

HOW TO TAPE A SIGN TO THE WALL
(without ruining the wall)

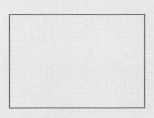 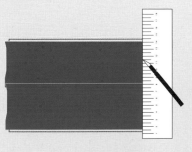 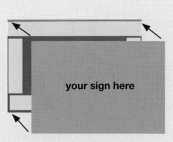

your sign here

1. *In pencil, lightly trace around your sign on the surface where it will be installed.*

2. *Apply blue painter's tape to the wall inside your pencil lines. (Painter's tape won't pull off the paint later.) With an X-Acto knife and a ruler, trim off the extra tape, leaving a neat blue rectangle that's a hair smaller than your sign. Erase pencil lines.*

3. *Place strips of double-stick tape around the edges of the blue rectangle, and then carefully position the sign on top of the rectangle. Press firmly.*

NOTE: If you don't plan to be at your place of employment for long enough to see the sign removed, skip Step 2. But be warned: double-stick tape will seriously damage your paint job over time. This technique was developed for use in a major New York City art museum. It works.

SOFT SELL *Personal feelings dominate social media.*

WHY NO ONE WANTS TO READ YOUR BLOG

I have a friend. Let's call her Ashley. She has a blog. Let's call it "My-BetterBody." Here she records her personal workout goals and details her Extreme StepMaster achievements. Ashley uses a special utility that translates her calorie intake and exercise output into appetizing pie charts for virtual consumption by her personal trainer, her grandmother in Phoenix, and her neighbor's dog.

The blog, Ashley tells me, keeps her on the Nordic track towards a slimmer, tighter tomorrow. "Now that I've told the whole world I'm going to work out, I need to stick with my program," she confides. She also uses the blog to announce her participation in various races for various cures. And occasionally, she'll send out an email reminder to her closest friends (around 100 of us). "Updated my blog." "Check out my exercise photos." "Don't forget to sponsor me in the Mud Race for Minor Miracles."

In his book *Zero Comments*, Geert Lovink argues that blogs, the poster child of social media, are not really that social after all. Whereas early listservs sent postings by many people to many people, most blogs have one author, who speaks to a public largely of her own imagining. Whereas the email lists of yore addressed topics of special interest (early music, late Nietzsche, mid-century modern), the subject of most personal blogs is, well, the person: her doodles and her diets, her children's lesser achievements and her kitchen's greater failures. The old listservs emulated the café or the open office; the blogs of today are more like living rooms, bourgeois broadcasting stations where private lives get uploaded with the shameless exactitude of a lap dancing accountant. Blogging, Lovink writes, is all about "me," not "we."

"Blog" is a contraction of "web log," and its form favors the list, whether it's a list of favorite sites or a catalog of done-that's and to-do's. Media scholar and early blogger Peter Krapp finally exited from the blogosphere with a posting entitled: "Top Ten Reasons I Don't Blog Anymore." The last reason? "Because Top Ten Lists Suck."

I don't exercise much, although I work up a sweat walking from my house to my car. I do, however, blog. This book began as a blog, with postings authored not only by Ellen and me, but by a widening circle of friends, strangers, and the occasional lonely Viagra salesman. We've used the blog in order to test ideas and to draft the seedlings of chapters in 300 word bursts. Although Design-Your-Life.org explores the arts of self-fashioning, it rarely dwells on the merely personal. It is more porch than parlor.

The best blogs, like the early listservs, lay claim to a focused topic that just might draw a readership, whether it's the rhetoric of the Internet, eighteenth-century cookery, or etiquette in the age of commuting. A blog, however, doesn't have to consist of essays on a theme. A blog may look like a diary, but it's really a just a database. It can be used to build a group or individual project, explore a specific subject area, present a portfolio of work, or serve as an on-line sketchbook. Blogs can facilitate wedding planning as well as divorce proceedings. And, yes, it can be used for calorie counting. Just don't expect a lot of comments. **JL**

Writing Matters

Blogging need not reduce your writing to slovenly drivel. If you blog with care, writing online can actually improve your style.

GETTING STARTED If the idea of having your own blog turns you into stone or jelly, try writing a reply to someone else's blog or posting a review on Amazon.

PERFECTING THE MIDDLE STYLE Blogging lies somewhere between the polished syntax of epic verse and the rough music of text messaging. Blogging can help relax your tone and reveal your voice. Avoid too many contractions and colloquialisms, though: @TEOTD, ("at the end of the day"), abbreviations diminish both rhythm and accessibility. So do spelling errors.

OPPORTUNITIES FOR REVISION Blogging can be a moment in a journey towards more formal writing. Try drafting essays in a more private space such as a Word doc or a less traveled blog or web account. Edit for clarity and concision when you post more publicly. If you plan to publish your work in another form, revise again. And again.

Top Ten Things to Do with a Blog

There are many kinds of blogging software, requiring varying degrees of skill and allowing different levels of customization. The easiest are free services such as Blog-Spot or LiveJournal, which provides you with templates, server space, and a web address, and require minimal software savvy. The photosharing site Flickr also has a blog feature. Here are some project ideas that look outwards, not inwards.

1. Write a book. Use blog entries to draft an abstract, develop examples, record data, and get feedback. Group projects like cookbooks and family histories as well as single-authored books on a special topic (cooking with your eyes closed, fun with matchbooks, the art of cheese carving) can be built through a blog.

2. Start a reading club. Choose a book. Tag some friends. Pose a question. (But don't give away the ending.)

3. Teach a class. Ask students to post essays or informal reading responses to a blog. Or, use the blog to post assignments, updates, and class photos.

4. Build a portfolio. Store pictures, writing, or links to projects and reports for use by possible employers, graduate programs, clients, or editors.

5. Curate an exhibition. From displays of children's art for a local school to cataloguing photographs by a group of fellow travelers, blogs can be used to organize and post a collective body of work.

6. Brand a business. Whether your gig involves pet sitting, head hunting, or basket weaving, a blog can help you establish and communicate with a client base.

7. Form a support group. Survived head lice? Addicted to bottled water? Fond of ferrets? Use a blog to build a community.

8. Share your expertise. Do you specialize in folding socks, drawing with your teeth, or building your own yo-yos? Use blog entries to give instructions, provide examples, and store information.

9. Plan a wedding. Unlike marriage, a blog need not entail a long-term commitment. Set up a blog in order to post gift registries, travel information, and the groom's baby pictures and sperm count.

10. Listen and learn. Don't just start conversations. Join a few, too. Read blogs, and leave comments —when you have something to say.

LETHAL WEAPON *Too many bullets will doom the best-intentioned presenter.*

DODGING BULLETS (IN POWERPOINT)

I once attended a presentation by designer Bruce Mau. It was after lunch, a tough time to keep people's attention. Mau structured his talk around a list of points from his personal design manifesto. Each point was as short, sweet, and crisp as an intellectual fortune cookie. "Number 14. Don't be cool." "Number 20. Be careful to take risks." "Number 25. Don't clean your desk." Instead of rolling out his points in numerical order, he released them in a seemingly random sequence (8, 2, 5, 30...). The audience was transfixed.

In contrast to Mau's clever take on conventions are those deadly scenarios where presenters drone on through screen after screen of dreary text, reading aloud word for word. Multimedia often serves more as a crutch for the speaker than as an illuminating communication with an audience. PowerPoint has gotten a bad rap on account of the ugly and inane stuff people do with it: huge logos and toxic gradients; cheesy transitions and stale clip art; and text—lots and lots of it, arranged in endless lists of bullet points. Shoot me now.

Yet PowerPoint and its more elegant sister Keynote (for the Mac) are not inherently evil—they simply have been abused and over-used to the point of exhaustion. Mastery of this basic software is a required skill in many lines of work. PowerPoint files can be printed, posted, and emailed as well as projected on a screen. They enable collaboration and multimedia authoring. What's more, PowerPoint is so easy to learn, even your boss could do it.

Long the butt of cruel humor, PowerPoint is undergoing a bit of a renaissance. Pecha Kucha (pronounced *pet-shah coot-shah*) is a presentation format that's sweeping the world. Each speaker in a Pecha Kucha event shows twenty slides, which are timed to display automatically for twenty seconds each, yielding about six and a half minutes on stage. Devised by a pair of Tokyo-based architects, Pecha Kucha keeps every speaker at an event moving along quickly and fluidly.

Following are some suggestions for how to create audience-friendly presentations—and what to avoid. EL

The Meatballer: Marketing Campaign

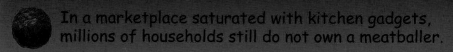

● In a marketplace saturated with kitchen gadgets, millions of households still do not own a meatballer.

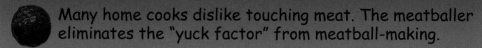

● Many home cooks dislike touching meat. The meatballer eliminates the "yuck factor" from meatball-making.

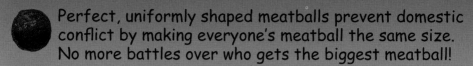

● Perfect, uniformly shaped meatballs prevent domestic conflict by making everyone's meatball the same size. No more battles over who gets the biggest meatball!

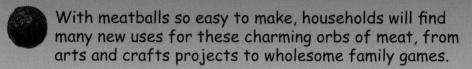

● With meatballs so easy to make, households will find many new uses for these charming orbs of meat, from arts and crafts projects to wholesome family games.

don't

● Don't overload your slides with mountains of text. The only thing duller than listening to someone read a speech is to follow along on screen while they are reading it.

● Don't put long lists of bullet points on a single screen. Present no more than three points on a single slide, and keep them short.

● Don't use cute or curly typefaces. The font used above (Comic Sans) tries to look casual and handmade—and yet PowerPoint presentations are carefully planned and scripted. Save spontaneity for your oral delivery. Keep your electronic presentation calm and authoritative.

● Don't use complex, distracting backgrounds. If your presentation is dull, a rainbow-colored gradient won't make it more interesting. For showing your presentation on screen, a black background with white text is considered ideal—the background disappears, allowing the text to float. But if your users will be printing out your slides, use a white background instead, for a "greener," toner-saving print job.

● Don't produce an important document in PowerPoint when another format would be more effective. For example, your company's emergency evacuation plan may be better delivered on a one-page PDF than in a fifty-slide PowerPoint show.

WHAT IS A BULLET?
In typography, a bullet serves to draw the eye to short chunks of text. Any decorative character can be used as a bullet—a dot, a diamond, even a meat-ball. Long bullet lists work well on a printed page, but short ones are recommended for screen presentations.

Pose questions.

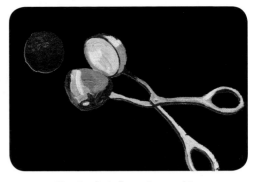

Use simple, informative graphics.

Combine image and text.

Let them know when it's almost over.

do

● Do anchor your thoughts with short chunks of text, underscoring your subject matter for the audience. Use text to inspire and provoke people, not to impress them or lull them to sleep.

● Do ask questions. Posing a concise and provocative query on screen can build interest and suspense.

● Do choose a clear, readable font and deploy it in consistent sizes, large enough to read from a distance. If colleagues are going to download or edit your presentation, you will need to use a typeface that they have access to, such as Helvetica, Times Roman, Verdana, or Georgia.

● Do use images to illuminate and demonstrate your ideas. Add some "show" to your "tell."

● Do consider alternative tools. Use page layout software such as InDesign to create beautiful, precise slides; export a PDF for your presentation. Other presentation media include slide shows set up in Flickr, blogs or websites that the audience can respond to later, and DVDs designed with a nicely crafted menu. Or, skip electronic media altogether and give your audience a paper handout; they can write on it and take it home.

WHY YOU SHOULD WRITE YOUR OWN MANIFESTO

1. Because no one else is going to write it for you.

2. Because it's shorter than a novel.

3. Because words ending in –o sound sophisticated.

4. Examples: *groucho, ergo, cappuccino, placebo, milano, motto.*

5. Exceptions: *righto, yummo, memo.*

6. A manifesto is not a memo. It is a declaration of independence.

7. If a manifesto is good enough for a revolution, why not write one for a bake sale, boycott, or bar mitzvah?

8. Tongue-tied? Dumbstruck? Brainstorm with a group or borrow talking points from favorite examples.

HOW TO MAKE A MANIFESTO

Karl Marx had one. The Unibomber had one. When Thomas Jefferson drafted the Declaration of Independence, he wrote the manifesto that defined the American Revolution. In 1909, F. T. Marinetti's Futurist Manifesto launched the idea of art as a branded public enterprise.

Designers seem especially drawn to manifestos. A well-written manifesto is like a well-designed product. It communicates directly, it is broken into functional parts, and it has elements of poetry and surprise. And drafting one is more like writing an ad than a novel.

Bruce Sterling's "Manifesto of January 3, 2000" helped galvanize the contemporary green movement. In addition to demanding the overhaul of all social, political, and military systems, Sterling pushed designers to create *"intensely glamorous environmentally sound products; entirely new objects of entirely new materials; replacing material substance with information; a new relationship between the cybernetic and the material."* (iPhone, anyone?) More recently, Emily Pilloton's "(Anti) Manifesto: A Call to Action for Humanitarian (Product) Design" uses snappy subject headings to draw readers in and give them something to remember: *"Taking the 'product' out of product design." "Activism over academics." "Design is the new micro-loan."*

Ulla-Maaria Mutanen's "Draft Craft Manifesto" talks about the social phenomena that result from the craft impulse: *"Learning techniques brings people together. This creates online and offline communities of practice." "Craft-oriented people seek opportunities to discover interesting things and meet their makers. This creates marketplaces."*

Mutanen's manifesto also talks about the importance of tools to crafting—not just physical tools like needles and band saws, but intellectual tools like recipes and tutorials. A manifesto is, in the end, a tool. It helps the writer articulate a point of view, shaping and compressing theories and beliefs into an essential and directed form, and it helps readers discover their own position. It's a tool that anyone can make, share, and use. **EL & JL**

N.I.C.E.

NEIGHBORS INCENSED ABOUT CANINE EXCREMENT

N.I.C.E. was established in order to organize concerned citizens around the growing problem of uncollected canine feces left in the Springfield Commons by a small number of inconsiderate dog owners.

Our N.I.C.E. mission is:
- *to raise awareness about the unsightly and unhygienic character of canine feces;*
- *to encourage interspecies courtesy and thoughtfulness;*
- *to collect funds for installing discrete doggie bag dispensers around the perimeter of our park.*

Please be N.I.C.E. with us at www.blogspot.com/nice

MEMO OR MANIFESTO? Imagine a group of neighbors angry about dog owners who don't pick up after their pets. These concerned citiizens could choose to be polite about their problem, writing a calm and quiet memo, or they could state their goals with the intensity that they feel, turning a dull plea for common courtesy into a blunt call for action.

DOG SH*T BRIGADE

We declare the following truths to be self-evident:

We love dogs but not their sh*t.

Rats eat it.

People step in it.

Kids shouldn't have to wear hazmat suits to the park.

We want dog sh*t out of our park and off our shoes. We will fight dog sh*t by any means necessary: signs, t-shirts, doggie bag dispensers, citizen arrests, Really Direct Mailings, and more.

Join now at www.blogspot.com/dogsh*t

TART
*Be quick, clear, and real.
Don't be bland; have a voice.*

WHY THIS WORKS
*Bold name.
Simple typography.
Unvarnished truth.
Direct call to action.*

Design is *thinking*.
Design is *making*.
Design is *public*.
Design is *private*.
Design is *garbage*.
Design is *saving the world*.
Design is *communication*.
Design is *craft*.
Design is *technology*.
Design is *serving dinner*.
Design is *cleaning up*.
Design is *teaching your kids*.
Design is *making your bed*.
Design is *making money*.
Design is *saving time*.
Design is *branding*.
Design is *zoning*.
Design is *planning*.
Design is *a mess*.
Design is *changing*.
Design is *surprising*.
Design is *ordinary*.
Design is *everywhere*.

[MANIFESTO: ELLEN AND JULIA LUPTON]

READING LIST

We consulted numerous books, websites, and newspaper articles in the making of this book. We also got many ideas from our friends, family, and our ongoing blog, Design-Your-Life.org. Our main sources are listed here.

MOVING THE FURNITURE On the design of hospital rooms, see John Spohn, "Imagining a Better Hospital Room," http://www.healthcaredesignmagazine.com/ (accessed 7/21/08). On moveable furniture before modernity, see Witold Rybczynski, *Home: A Short History of an Idea* (Penguin: 1987).

LIVING ROOMS On the history of the parlor, see Thad Logan, *The Victorian Parlor* (Cambridge University Press, 2001) and Katherine Grier, *Culture and Comfort: People, Parlors, and Upholstery, 1850–1930* (University of Massachusetts Press, 1988). On new trends in living rooms, see David Keeps, "Dust off the Divan," *Los Angeles Times* (8/11/2005). On living rooms and conversation, see Ray Faulkner and Sarah Faulkner, *Inside Today's Home* (Henry Holt and Company, 1954). On home decor as personal therapy, see Maxwell Gillingham-Ryan, *Apartment Therapy: The Eight-Step Home Cure* (Bantam Books, 2006).

VIEW FINDINGS For modern curtain designs, see Petra Blaisse, *Inside Outside* (NAI Publishers, 2007), Matilda McQuaid, *Lilly Reich: Designer and Architect* (Museum of Modern Art, 1996), and Mary Davis Gillies, *Popular Home Decoration* (Wise & Co., 1946). Our picture-hanging tips were inspired in part by Gillies. On Mary Bright, see Williams Weathersby, Jr., "Architectonic draperies by the Mary Bright Studio give new meaning to the phrase 'curtain wall,'" *Architectural Record* (June 2005): 198-201; William L. Hamilton, "A Curtain Maker Who Challenges the View," *New York Times* (7/25/2002); and William L. Hamilton, "Mary Bright, 48, Curtain Maker Who Used Unorthodox Materials," *New York Times* (11/30/2002), obituary. Mary Bright illustration based on a photo by Peter Page.

PORCHES See Michael Dolan, *The American Porch: An Informal History of an Informal Place* (Lyons Press, 2002), Renee Kahn and Ellen Meagher, *Preserving Porches*, (Henry Holt and Company, 1984), and Jocelyn Hazelwood Donlon, *Swinging in Place: Porch Life in Southern Culture* (University of North Carolina Press, 2001). Joe Robinson evaluates the New Urban porch in "Say Hello to an Old Friend," *Los Angeles Times* (10/12/ 2006). Image from Christopher Alexander, *A Pattern Language* (1977) reproduced by permission of Oxford University Press, Inc.

GETTING OUT OF THE HOUSE On the third place idea, see Ray Oldenburg, *Third Places: The Great Good Place* (Marlowe and Company, 1989; 1997). On latent and manifest functions, see R. K. Merton, *Social Theory and Social Structure* (The Free Press, 1968). On brandscaping, see Celia Lury, *Brands: The Logos of the Global Economy* (Routledge, 2004). On trends in home office work, see Ralph Gardner, Jr., "Home-Office Life and Its Discontents," *New York Times* (1/3/2008): D1, D7. Visit Paragraph at http://www.paragraphny.com (accessed 7/21/2008). On the work habits of Louis Auchincloss, see Larissa MacFarquhar, "East Side Story: How Louis Auchincloss Came to Terms with His World," *The New Yorker* (February 25, 2008): 54–63. *Craving the Buzz* illustration based on Edgar Degas, *L'Absinthe*, 1875–6; *Sweat Shop* loosely inspired by the posters of Henri de Toulouse Lautrec.

TOASTERS On the miracle of toast, see Harold McGee, *On Food and Cooking: The Science and Lore of the Kitchen* (Scribner, 1984; 2004). View toasters online at the Cyber Toaster Museum (http://www.toaster.org/; accessed 7/21/2008).

KITCHEN COMPUTERS The Internet news site C|NET News.com closely covered the rise and fall of Internet appliances. See Ian Fried, "An icebox with your white box," October 10, 2002 (http://www.news.com/2100-1040-961619.html; accessed 7/21/2008). On integrating standard computer equipment into a high-end kitchen, see Kathleen Hacket, "Hidden Assets." *Martha Stewart Living* (January 2008): 96–103. For a skeptical analysis of media fridges, see Caslon Analytics, "Internet Fridges," http://www.caslon.com.au/fridgenote1.htm (accessed 7/21/2008). In "The Networked Home," Alladi Venkatesh, Erik Kruse, and Eric Chuan-Fong Shih address the use of design to integrate social, physical, and technological spaces (*Cognition, Technology, and Work* [2003] 5:23–32). On the mobile phone as "mobile home," see David Morley, *Media, Modernity and Technology: The Geography of the New* (Routledge, 2007). On can openers and other technologies for the kitchen, see Brian S. Alexander. *Atomic Kitchen: Gadgets and Inventions for Yesterday's Cook* (Collectors Press, 2004). On housework as make-work, see Ruth Schwartz Cohen. *More Work for Mother: The Ironies of Household Technology from the Open Hearth to the Microwave* (Basic Books, 1983). See also Ellen Lupton, *Mechanical Brides: Women and Machines from Home to Office* (Princeton Architectural Press, 1996).

BAGGAGE CLAIMS Few people have the courage to speak out against roller bags. One of them is Seth Johnson, who published an OpEd piece called "Hell on Wheels" in the *New York Times* (12/20/2007).

BEDS AND PILLOWS On Auden's housekeeping, see Rebecca Mead, "Ink a Home-Ec Bible and W. H. Auden," *The New Yorker*, March 20, 2000.

HONOR BARS On market-driven environmentalism, see John Thakara, *In the Bubble: Designing in a Complex World* (MIT Press, 2006).

BRAS There's no substitute for being fitted in person by a professional bra fitter. The online lingerie shop HerRoom compiles expert advice for shoppers who'd rather stay at home (http://www.herroom.com/bra-fitting-advice,901,30.html; accessed 7/22/2008). Bra designer Beverly Johnson provides an inside view of the bra industry and how bras fit on her blog (http://bra-makers.blogspot.com/2006/04/bra-that-fits.html; 7/22/2008); our drawings of good and bad fit are inspired by her diagrams. See also Beatrice Fontanel, *Support and Seduction: The History of Corsets and Bras* (Abradale Press, 2001). *Ain't No Mountain High Enough* illustration based on Caspar David Friedrich's *The Wanderer Above the Sea of Fog*, 1818. *Nice Lady; Scary Underwear* illustration based on an advertising image for Spirella, 1958; posted on Ivy Leaf's Corsetry Compendium, http://www.corsetiere.net/Spirella/problems.htm#Gir (accessed 7/22/2008).

BABY CARROTS AND OTHER FOOD MYSTERIES On the birth of baby carrots, see Elizabeth Weise, *USA Today*, "Digging the Baby Carrot," 8.11/2004 (http://www.usatoday.com/life/lifestyle/2004-08-11-baby-carrot_x.htm; accessed 7/21/2008). On corn and the American diet, see Michael Pollan, *The Omnivore's Dilemma: A Natural History of Four Meals* (Penguin, 2006). On lettuce, see "Bagged salads: the yuck factor," *Consumer Reports*, 2006 (http://www.consumerreports.org/cro/food/food-shopping/fruits-vegetables/bagged-salads/bagged-salads-11-06/overview/1106_salad_ov_1.htm; accessed 7/21/2008). On chicken, see Roger Horowitz, *Putting Meat on the Table: Taste, Technology, Transformation* (The Johns Hopkins University Press, 2006). *Gateway Vegetables* illustration inspired by a photograph by Kelly Cline, iStockphoto.

AFFORDANCES On affordances and ecology, see James J. Gibson, "The Theory of Affordances," in R. Shaw & J. Bransford (eds.), *Perceiving, Acting and Knowing* (Erlbaum, 1977), pp. 67–82. On the affordances of everyday objects, see Donald Norman, *The Design of Everyday Things* (Basic Books, 1988). On the broken window theory applied to housekeeping, see Cheryl Mendelson, *Home Comforts: The Art and Science of Keeping House* (Scribner, 1999). Jennifer Tobias wrote about the "archaeology" of bathroom stall toilet paper dispensers on our blog, http://design-your-life.org/blog.php?id=79 (accessed July 22, 2008).

PILES On the significance of stacking, see Malcolm Gladwell, "The Social Life of Paper," *The New Yorker*, March 25, 2002. See also Eric Abrahamson and David H. Freedman, *A Perfect Mess: The Hidden Benefits of Disorder* (Little, Brown, 2006). On the paperless office and other fictions of the digital age, see John Seely Brown and Paul Duguid, *The Social Life of Information* (Harvard Business School Press, 2002). On life hacking, see Clive Thompson, "Meet the Life Hackers," *New York Times* (10/ 16/2005). Rendering of Al Gore's desk loosely reconstructed from a photograph by Steve Pyke for *Time* Magazine, May 2007.

MULTITASKING In *The Humane Interface: New Directions for Designing Interactive Systems* (Addison Wesley, 2000), Jef Raskin applies studies of human attention to problems in computer interface design. On continuous partial attention, see Linda Stone, http:// continuouspartialattention.jot.com/WikiHome (accessed 7/22/2008).

PROCRASTINATION For time management in the new millenium, we consulted Lisa Nakone, *Organizing for Your Brain Type: Finding Your Own Solution to Managing Time, Paper, and Stuff* (St. Martin's Griffin, 2005), Gina Trapani, *Lifehacker: 88 Tech Tricks to Turbocharge Your Life* (Wiley, 2007); David Allen, *Getting Things Done: The Art of Stress-Free Productivity* (Viking, 2001). 43 Folders.com is a family of websites hosted by Merlin Mann and devoted to lifehacking and productivity (accessed 7/22/2008). On lists, see John Hodgman, *The Areas of My Expertise* (E.P. Dutton, 2005). Goodreads.com invites readers to list and review books (accessed 7/22/2008). Learning how *not* to read just might save you some time. See Pierre Bayard, *How to Talk about Books You Haven't Read* (Bloomsbury, 2007).

SHOE WARS On our blog, a shoes-off post contributed by Michellel Qureshi has attracted dozens of impassioned responses over a several-year period; see http://www.design-your-life. org/blog.php?id=62 (accessed 6/4/2008). Similar conflicts can be observed at http://www. apartmenttherapy.com/ny/good-questions/good-questions-is-shoes-off-at-a-party-proper-006082 (accessed June 7, 2008). Joyce Wadler writes about "extreme hosting" in "Welcome...Oh, but Don't Sit There," *New York Times* (November 30, 2006). Martha Stewart is a firm advocate of shoes-off policies; see http://www.marthastewart. com/article/off-with-their-shoes (accessed 6/3/2008). Out-moded manners taken from Sophie Hadida, *Manners for Millions* (Sun Dial Press, 1932).

WORKING MOTHERS On motherhood and its discontents, see Judith Warner, *Perfect Madness: Motherhood in the Age of Anxiety* (Riverhead Trade, 2006). The NICD Study of Early Child

Care and Youth Development, published by the National Institute of Child Health and Human Development in 2007, found that children who spend significant time in daycare or preschool before kindergarten are more likely to display disruptive behavior in the classroom later; http:// secc.rti.org/; accessed 7/21/2008. *Working Father* image based on a photograph by Stephen Morris, iStockphoto.

MISGIVINGS Muhammad Yunus describes the evolution of micro-lending in his memoir and manifesto, *Banker to the Poor: Micro-Lending and the Battle Against World Poverty* (Public Affairs, 1999). On peer-to-peer lending in developing countries, see Jodi Dean, Jon W. Anderson, and Geert Lovink, *Reformatting Politics: Information Technology and Global Civil Society* (Routledge 2006). Landscape backgrounds in the illustrations were taken from a cardboard painting purchased at a yard sale; artist unknown.

STRANGE STUFFIES Our profile of "the self-starter" is based on the career of Jen Bennett Gubicza (sweetestpea.com, accessed 7/22/2008). Our profile of "the graphic novelist" is based on Aranzi Aronzo, *The Cute Book* (Vertical, 2007). The "mainstreamer" is based on David Horvath and Sun-Min Kim, creators of Ugly Dolls, http://www.uglydolls.com/ (accessed 7/22/2008). The "organic intellectual" is inspired by Tsia Carson at Supernturale.com (accessed 7/222/2008). *Mazzles* portrait is based on a photo posted on Crafters.org (http://www. craftster.org/forum/index.php?topic=128500. msg1245924#msg1245924; accessed 7/22/2008).

FLOWERS On Victorian flower symbolism, see Beverly Seaton, *The Language of Flowers: A History* (University of Virginia Press, 1995). See also Bastiaan Meeuse and Sean Morris, *The Sex Life of Flowers* (Faber and Faber, 1984).

HOMELAND SECURITY Wendy Mogel argues for a more relaxed parenting approach in *The Blessing of a Skinned Knee: Using Jewish Teachings to Raise Self-Reliant Children* (Penguin, 2001). Audrey van Buskirk comments on car seats in "Riding right's tough to do," *The Portland Tribune* (11/27/2007). On bike-riding and the new childhood, see L. J. Williamson, "Life Support," published in the *Los Angeles Times*, 2007; reprinted in the *Pittsburgh*

Post Gazette (4/3/2007; http://www.post-gazette.
com/pg/07093/774604-51.stm; accessed
7/21/2008). For car seat assistance, see the
Partners for Child Passenger Safety, Children's
Hospital of Philadelphia (http://www.chop.edu/
consumer/jsp/division/generic.jsp?id=77971;
accessed 7/21/2008). On crib safety, see http://
www.cpsc.gov/cpscpub/pubs/5049.html
(accessed 7/21/2008) and Heather Corley, "Crib
Bumper Pads" (http://babyproducts.about.
com/od/recallsandsafety/a/bumpersafety.htm;
accessed 7/21/2008).

THE PERMANENT HOLIDAY For a literary
anthropology of holidays, see the classic book
by C. L. Barber, *Shakespeare's Festive Comedy*
(Princeton: 1972). On Thanksdriving, see http://
www.bts.gov/publications/america_on_the_go/
us_holiday_travel/ (accessed 7/21/2008).
For tampon angels (and menorahs, too), visit
Tamponcrafts.com (accessed 7/21/2008). On
trends in fall retailing, see Stuart Elliott, "After
Labor Day, Go Directly to Halloween," *New York
Times* 9/17/2007. On carbon fasting, see http://
www.tearfund.org/Churches/Carbon+Fast.htm
(accessed 7/21/2008). *Silent Fright* illustration
inspired by Edward Munch's *The Scream*, 1893.

SERVING SUGGESTIONS On planning a buffet,
see http://www.divinedinnerparty.com/buffet-
table-setting.html (accessed 7/21/2008). On the
politics of table shapes, see Klaus Herdeg, *The
Decorated Diagram: Harvard Architecture and
the Failure of the Bauhaus Legacy* (MIT Press,
1983), p.27. On matchmaking for builders, see
Rosie Millard, "Speed Dating for Architects and
Developers." *Sunday Times* (London), 2/24/2008.
On snap judgments, see Malcolm Gladwell, *Blink*
(Backbay Books, 2003). On tableware, see Sarah
D. Coffin, Ellen Lupton, and Barbara Bloemink,
*Feeding Desire: Design and the Tools of the Table,
1500–2005* (Assouline, 2006).

GARAGE BRANDING On pink ribbons, see
Samantha King, *Pink Ribbons: Breast Cancer
and the Politics of Philanthropy* (University of
Minnesota Press, 2006). On brands, see Adam
Arvidsson, *Brands: Meaning and Value in Media
Culture* (Routledge, 2006); and Henry Jenkins,
Fans, Bloggers, and Gamers (NYU: 2006). On
MUJI, see Kenya Hara, *Designing Design* (Lars
Müller Publishers, 2007) and *MUJI: Brands A to*

Z (Page One Publishing, 2007). See also Ellen
Lupton, ed., *D.I.Y.: Design It Yourself* (Princeton
Architectural Press, 2006).

FONTS For more on fonts, see Ellen Lupton,
*Thinking with Type: A Critical Guide for Designers,
Writers, Editors, and Students* (Princeton
Architectural Press, 2004). On Futura, see
Christopher Burke, *Paul Renner: The Art of
Typography* (Princeton Architectural Press, 1998).

BLOGGING On the antisocial side of social media,
see Geert Lovink, *Zero Comments: Blogging and
Critical Internet Culture* (Routledge, 2008). Peter
Krapp's blog is http://distraction-economy.org/
(accessed 7/21/2008). Other blogs referenced
in this essay include 18thccuisine.blogspot.com,
www.virtualpolitik.blogspot.com/ and http://www.
munimanners.com/ (all accessed 7/21/2008).
Virtualpolitik.com became a book: see Elizabeth
Losh, *Virtualpolitik* (MIT Press, 2008).

POWERPOINT Read Bruce Mau's "Incomplete
Manifesto for Growth" (1998) at http://www.
brucemaudesign.com/manifesto.html (accessed
7/22/2008). For a critique of PowerPoint, see
Edward Tufte, *The Cognitive Style of PowerPoint*
(Graphics Press, 2003).

SIGNS OF FAILURE Daniel Pink has lectured
on the idea of emotionally intelligent
signage; see http://www.youtube.com/
watch?v=9NZOt6BkhUg (accessed 7/21/2008).
The Society for Environmental Graphic Design is
dedicated to signage and exhibition design; visit
http://www.segd.org/ (accessed 7/21/2008).

MANIFESTOS On the history of manifestos, see
Martin Puchner, *Poetry of the Revolution: Marx,
Manifestos, and the Avant-Gardes* (Princeton
University Press, 2005). Read these contemporary
manifestos: Bruce Sterling, "The Manifesto of
January 3, 2000" http://www.viridiandesign.org/
manifesto.html; Emily Pilloton, "(Anti)Manifesto:
A Call to Action for Humanitarian (Product)
Design," http://www.core77.com/blog/featured_
items/project_h_design_antimanifesto_a_call_
to_action_for_humanitarian_product_design_by_
emily_pilloton_9668.asp; Ulla-Maaria Mutanen,
"Draft Craft Manifesto," http://ullamaaria.
typepad.com/hobbyprincess/2005/03/draft_craft_
man.html (all accessed 7/21/2008).

ACKNOWLEDGMENTS

This book was composed in the factory-studios of our houses and workplaces, supplemented by the occasional café and airplane. We couldn't have written this book without the provocation and support provided by many people.

We met our editor, BJ Berti, after a lecture at Urban Center Books, New York City, in 2006. She introduced herself and proposed working with St. Martin's Press on this project. Her advocacy and guidance have never faltered, and we are thrilled to be building a new relationship with one of the world's premiere publishers.

Two "working fathers" deserve special thanks. Abbott Miller has provided an ongoing education in living with design; he is our muse. Kenneth Reinhard has responded to chapters with chuckles and the occasional quizzical eyebrow, provided snappy subtitles on short notice, and helped supervise four kids and two cats so that we could keep writing.

Our children, Jay and Ruby Miller, and Hannah, Isabel, Lucy, and Eliot Reinhard, provided the comic relief and the daily challenges that made this book worth writing.

Our parents, Bill and Shirley Lupton, and Mary Jane Lupton and Kenneth Baldwin, have supported our ventures since 1963. This book is no exception. We especially thank Bill for making life in Baltimore an ongoing design experiment, and Mary Jane for demonstrating a life of letters and creativity.

From Baltimore and New York, we thank Inna Alesina, Joy Hayes, Claudia Matzko, Jennifer Cole Phillips, Marybeth Shaw, Michelle Qureshi, and Jennifer Tobias for their friendship and ideas. From California, we thank Julka Almquist, Ava Arndt, Suzanne Bolding, Barbara Cohen, Vivian Folkenflik, Steve Franklin, Helene Hecht, Anna Kornbluh, Peter Krapp, Catherine Liu, Elizabeth Losh, Lynn Mally, Sanjoy Mazumdar, Mia McIver, Alladi Venkatesh, and Jennifer Hardy Williams for services ranging from bibliography and essay ideas to babysitting and virtual massages.

One of the great pleasures of creating this book was producing the illustrations. Although Ellen studied painting as a student at The Cooper Union, she gave it up for design and hadn't picked up a paintbrush for nearly twenty years until Nicholas Blechman asked her to create an illustration for *The New York Times Book Review* in Spring 2007. That experience, which was followed by additional *NYT* commissions, triggered the visual concept of this book. The work of many artists stimulated our thinking, including Maira Kalman, who makes picture books for adults, and Richard Scarry, whose visual dictionaries were among our very first (and most treasured) possessions.

Brett Leveridge at Media Bistro and Jane Delury at University of Baltimore helped us focus our writing, as did many friends who looked at early drafts of this book.

Various institutions have provided rich intellectual contexts for our work; we thank the Headlands Center for the Arts (Marin County, Caifornia), the Design Alliance at the University of California, Irvine, Kippy Stroud's Acadia Summer Arts Program, Princeton Architectural Press, *ReadyMade* magazine, Maryland Institute College of Art, and Cooper-Hewitt, National Design Museum, Smithsonian Institution. — *Ellen and Julia Lupton*

INDEX